Railway Memories N...

PONTEF...
CASTLEFO...D &
KNOTTINGLEY

Peter Cookson & Steve Chapman

BELLCODE BOOKS
21 DALE AVENUE
TODMORDEN
WEST YORKSHIRE OL14 6BA

Edited by Steve Chapman

Printed by the Amadeus Press Ltd.,
Cleckheaton, West Yorks.

Above: A once familiar sight all over the Castleford area, the small but powerful tank engines that worked tirelessly on its many colliery railways, many of them built in nearby Leeds by such manufacturers as the Hunslet Engine Co., Hudswell Clarke and Manning Wardle. Here, 0-6-0 saddletank *Bawtry*, Hunslet No. 1698 built in 1932, recently overhauled and wearing a smart new lined green livery, stands with a line of wagons at Wheldale Colliery on 8th April, 1970. *Robert Anderson*

Frontispiece: One of the Aspinall 0-6-0s introduced by the Lancashire & Yorkshire Railway in 1889, No.52305 from 53E Goole shed, pollutes the atmosphere as it hauls a Wakefield-bound class H Through Freight between Pontefract Monkhill and Tanshelf during the mid to late 1950s. Notice how neat and tidy the lineside was in those days compared with today's often unkempt and overgrown infrastructure. *Peter Cookson*

INTRODUCTION

Pontefract, Castleford and Knottingley may not at first seem all that significant in railway terms - but they are.

Exactly 170 years after Matthew Murray and John Blenkinsop set the world's first commercially viable steam locomotive to work hauling coal from Middleton Colliery to the banks of the River Aire in Leeds, one of the country's very last commercially working steam locomotives was doing the same job in Castleford, just ten miles along the same river.

Over in Pontefract, once the metropolis of West Yorkshire, one of the town's three stations was situated on one of the nation's prime cross-country routes, seeing some of the longest distance passenger trains and some of the heaviest freight trains hauled by the country's biggest engines.

Knottingley, always a key railway junction, has grown in railway stature through its role in feeding the nation's insatiable appetite for electricity.

Railway Memories No.15 shows how this area once saw the full range of trains from long-distance cross-country and cross-Pennine expresses to humble but vital trips pottering from colliery yard to colliery yard.

It also shows stations before they were stripped to little more than bus stops, yards before they were ripped up, and colliery lines which provided their own endless fascination into the 1980s.

It also shows how this area has retained some railway interest. In the 1950s there were no active locomotive depots in this area but in 2002 there were two just a mile or so apart.

Knottingley station has shrunk somewhat since 26th April, 1958 when it was graced by A1 Pacific No. 60157 *Great Eastern* **at the head of Ian Allan's Pennine Limited railtour from King's Cross. Apart from the size of the station then, note the huge water tank up on the left.** *Peter Cookson*

SETTING THE SCENE

Set amid gently rolling hills divided by the Aire and Calder rivers are possibly the most historically interesting communities in West Yorkshire.

Until very recently, that same area also had one of Yorkshire's most fascinating railway and industrial landscapes - if not the prettiest!

It is amazing now to think that in 1982 Castleford was home to one of Britain's very last commercially working steam locomotives, back where it all began, hauling coal from colliery to river staithes - exactly 170 years after Matthew Murray's locomotive had first hauled coal from the Middleton Colliery in Leeds to the banks of the self same river Aire.

Until the 1990s, Castleford was one of Britain's premier coal mining centres but its greatest industry is now just a part of its great history. Founded nearly 2,000 years ago when the Romans built a fort to guard the point where Deer Street, their road to York, crossed the river, it grew into the large settlement of Lagentium, now regarded as one of Britain's most important Roman archaeological sites. One of Yorkshire's oldest communities, Castleford also boasted such traditional industries as chemicals, pottery, glass and brick making.

At the heart of this land of hills and rivers, where industry, agriculture and history meet head-on, is Pontefract, meaning broken bridge and once the metropolis of West Yorkshire. The huge castle which dominated this ancient market town was a royal seat but its past was so dark and sinister that around 300 years ago the townsfolk successfully petitioned the king to have it demolished. Pontefract became best known for its racecourse and the local cash crop that became a major industry - liquorice.

Knottingley goes back to Anglo-Saxon times when it was founded by the Cnotta people. Its traditional industries were limestone quarrying and earthenware but with the opening of the Knottingley & Goole canal in 1826 it became an inland port with several boat building yards. Since then coal, chemicals, glass and the railway itself have become its main industries.

When the first main line railways reached this area in July, 1840, they put Castleford on a direct route to the Midlands and London. The York & North Midland Railway, with the ruthless Railway King George Hudson at its helm, came

from York to Burton Salmon, negotiated a short tunnel and bridged the River Aire at Fairburn, served Castleford with a station just north of the present one and then continued via Whitwood to Altfofts, just short of Normanton. There it joined the North Midland Railway from Leeds Hunslet Lane to Derby, which was being built at the same time. These lines were central to Hudson's grand vision, a main line between Yorkshire and London Euston. A Leeds-facing curve from Whitwood to the North Midland at Methley enabled through running between York, Castleford and Leeds.

The following year, the Manchester & Leeds Railway from Normanton to Wakefield and beyond to Manchester was fully complete, putting Castleford on the country's first trans-Pennine railway.

Pontefract and Knottingley joined the rapidly developing rail network seven years later when the Wakefield, Pontefract & Goole Railway whose name amply describes the route, was completed with the aim of forging a direct link between increasingly industrial West Yorkshire and the port of Goole. The WPG connected at Wakefield with the Manchester & Leeds, making a line all the way from Goole to Liverpool and by the time the Goole line opened in April, 1848, the two companies had merged to become the Lancashire & Yorkshire Railway.

Two months later, the L&Y completed the branch south from Knottingley to Askern, just north of Doncaster. There it met head-on with the Great Northern Railway which was pushing relentlessly northwards from London. Besides giving the L&Y access to Doncaster, running powers gave the GNR direct access to West Yorkshire and brought it within 18 miles of York.

With the L&Y set to open its line from Pontefract to the North Midland at Methley in autumn, 1849, the GNR would soon be able to run trains direct between London and Leeds. The stage was set for one of the most vicious manifestations of the bitter inter-company rivalries of the Railway Mania. Seeking to protect its own commercial interests, the Midland Railway which by this time had succeeded the North Midland, demanded that the GNR would not attempt to build its own line into Leeds. The GNR refused to give any such guarentee so the Midland threatened to stop all GN trains at Methley and extract

The York & North Midland Railway from York to Normanton was the first main line railway through this part of Yorkshire, passing as it did through Burton Salmon, Castleford and Whitwood.
Here, B16/2 4-6-0 No. 61435 approaches Castleford Gates level crossing with a southbound fully braked class C express goods from York. *Peter Cookson*
In 1964, No. 61435 was the last of these fine engines to be withdrawn but, like the rest of its classmates, sadly failed to find a place in preservation.

tolls from the passengers. This dispute culminated in the infamous "Methley Junction Incident." On the eve of the Pontefract-Methley line's proposed opening, GN officials, suspicious of the Midland, sent a light engine from Doncaster to Methley where the crew found that the points had been removed from the junction, action which could have derailed the first GN train.

While strongly opposing the Great Northern, Hudson's YNMR eventually sought to benefit from the GN's drive to reach York and set about building its Knottingley branch. Just three miles long from Burton Salmon to the L&Y at Knottingley, it completed the first East Coast route from London to York when opened for goods traffic in April, 1850. It included one of the more impressive railway structures in the area, the Brotherton tubular bridge over the River Aire, just north of Ferrybridge. This comprised two tubes 237ft long, one each to carry the Up and Down lines, both of which were fully opened to passenger traffic in October, 1852. Hudson's Euston route may have been well and truly

eclipsed but to reach York GNR trains had to run over YNM metals, at least until 1871 when the whole route lost its East Coast main line status to the newly completed Doncaster-Selby-York line.

In 1854 the YNMR merged with other companies in the North East to become the North Eastern Railway which eventually joined the GN and L&Y in joint operation of a line connecting Castleford and the north directly to the GN's expanding West Riding system. Opened to goods traffic in 1865 and passengers in 1869, the Methley Joint ran to the GN's newly completed Doncaster-Wakefield-Leeds route from connections with both the Whitwood and Pontefract lines at an increasingly complex Methley Junction.

By this time, advances in deep mining techniques were enabling rich underground coal measures around Castleford and Pontefract to be exploited to the full, and as the coalfield grew, so came the demand for more railways.

Foremost among these new lines was the NER's Leeds, Castleford & Pontefract Junction Railway

The Brotherton bridge over the River Aire was, and still is, one of the more impressive railway civil engineering structures of the area. In the early 20th century the tubular superstructure was replaced by a conventional girder bridge which is pictured in LNER days being traversed by Q6 0-8-0 No. 1250 heading a long goods train. Of particular interest is the North Eastern Railway slotted distant signal mounted on stonework. *Ernest Sanderson / Steve Chapman collection*

which ran to Castleford from the Leeds-Selby line at Garforth. Opened in 1878, it served a complex range of collieries around Kippax and Allerton Bywater. A curve from the new Castleford station to Cutsyke Junction, on the L&Y's Methley-Pontefract line, completed the full scheme in April, 1880.

One more main line was added to the network in 1879 when the NER and Midland railways opened the Swinton & Knottingley Joint from Ferrybridge, on the Burton Salmon-Knottingley branch, to the Leeds-Derby line at Swinton (Wath Road Junction.) It gave Pontefract its third and arguably most important station, at Baghill. The S&K was a switchback which needed considerable earthworks and gradients as steep as 1 in 150 with a couple of short bursts of 1 in 122/123.

Cutting 4.5 miles from the journey via Normanton and avoiding the need to change engines there, it formed the important York to Sheffield section of the main North East-South West route. A mile-long curve connecting Pontefract Baghill with Monkhill station on the

L&Y was added in 1880.

Among later additions to the local network was the three-mile Brackenhill Light Railway, opened in July, 1914 and connecting Hemsworth Colliery and a goods depot at Ackworth Moor Top with the S&K south of Pontefract via a 1 in 87 gradient. The goods only branch was worked by the NER but remained independent until becoming part of the London & North Eastern Railway in 1923. In March, 1915 the L&Y laid a curve between Knottingley South and East which enabled it to move coal to Goole direct from collieries around Doncaster.

These might have been the last acts but the combination of coal and electricity was to see more railways built in modern times. New works in the 1960s to serve the big new power stations at Ferrybridge, Eggborough and Drax included a mile-long line from Whitley Bridge to Eggborough power station, the reopening in 1970 of disused connections from the Goole line at Hensall Junction to a section of the Hull & Barnsley Railway reinstated to serve Drax power station, a new curve from Ferrybridge to the Goole line at Pontefract opened in 1965, and a new diesel locomotive and wagon depot at Knottingley.

Over the years, the area has been blessed with a fascinating selection of minor and industrial railways. Until the late 1960s/early 1970s an extensive network of lines served collieries near Swillington, between Castleford and Leeds. They connected Primrose Hill and other collieries to each other, to the Castleford-Garforth line and to staithes on the Aire & Calder Navigation. Wheldale and Fryston collieries at Castleford were connected by their own internal line which ran along the river bank and they too had a staithes branch. Connected to the L&Y and YNM lines at Whitwood were the Whitwood Colliery, briquette plant and chemical works, and next to Allerton Bywater Colliery, at the Castleford end of the Garforth branch, steam and diesel locomotives could be seen from the A656 road at the Coal Board's North Yorkshire Area central workshops. Going from Castleford towards Pontefract were Glasshoughton Colliery and coke works, the coke works still shunted in the mid-1970s by a delightful Hawthorn Leslie 0-6-0ST. Prince of

Wales Colliery, on the approach to Pontefract, was also steam worked around the same time. The coal industry in these parts kept steam alive 14 years after it disappeared from British Rail. In 1982 it was still possible to watch a steam locomotive shunting at Wheldale Colliery as modern High Speed Trains whizzed by with North East-South West InterCity services.

Over the years, the railways have undergone several changes in administration and ownership. In 1923, the many different railway companies were grouped into just four big undertakings. The L&Y and Midland went to the London Midland & Scottish Railway while the North Eastern and Great Northern joined the London & North Eastern Railway. These companies were nationalized on 1st January, 1948 and the railways brought under the control of British Railways which was divided into regions roughly following the lines of the old companies. Former LNER lines came under the North Eastern Region and LMS lines such as Wakefield-Goole went to the London Midland Region for operating purposes until 1957 when they were transferred to the NE Region. In 1965 British Railways

The coal industry's own railway operations kept working steam alive in the Castleford, Pontefract and Featherstone area for 14 years after it disappeared from main line British Railways. One of the more delightful engines to be seen working in later years was blue-liveried 0-6-0ST *Coal Products No 3*, built in 1923 by Hawthorn Leslie of Newcastle-upon-Tyne, works No. 3575. It was brought back into daily use at Glasshoughton coking works, Castleford, during the mid-1970s and in this view marshalls 16-ton mineral wagons next to the Methley-Pontefract line on 24th June, 1975. *Adrian Booth*

shortened its name to British Rail, and in 1967 the North Eastern and Eastern regions were merged to form a new Eastern Region managed from the NE headquarters in York.

During the 1990s the railways were privatised and are now run by a complicated host of companies. In 2002 the former North East-South West expresses were operated by Virgin Cross-Country and all local passenger services by Arriva Trains Northern. The main freight operator was English Welsh & Scottish Railway. Track, signalling, structures and control of operations were the responsibility of Railtrack but in October, 2001 the company was put under the control of government-appointed administrators and a year later these functions were handed to a replacement company called Network Rail.

Passenger services

The principal trains through Castleford, on the line from Burton Salmon to Normanton, were those between York and Manchester Victoria via the Lancashire & Yorkshire main line. The premier train of the 1950s was the 10.30am express from Liverpool Exchange to Newcastle and 5.10pm return from Newcastle, boasting a dining car, limited to 400 tons, and usually hauled by one of Liverpool Bank Hall shed's three Jubilee 4-6-0s, *Mars, Dauntless* or *Glorious*, or its un-named Patriot No. 45517. By the start of the 1960s it ran only between Liverpool and York.

Another interesting 1950s class A train was the unadvertised 6.55am SX from Normanton which took workers to the Thorp Arch ordnance factory near Wetherby. It left Castleford at 7.3am while the 5.32pm return reached Castleford at 6.34.

During the 1960s, passenger services on this line were heavily pruned and by summer, 1968 they consisted of three Manchester Victoria to York DMUs each way, two from Sowerby Bridge to York and one from York to Sowerby Bridge, one from Halifax to York, a seasonal Wakefield-Scarborough train each way and the 02.10 York-Manchester Victoria mail. On 5th January, 1970 the remaining passenger trains were withdrawn, ending Castleford's direct daily service to York and leaving the Castleford-Burton Salmon line to freight and parcels trains plus a few summer dated seaside excursions.

Castleford's premier train in the 1950s was the 10.30am dining car express from Liverpool Exchange to Newcastle, pictured at Castleford Central in 1959 with 27A Liverpool Bank Hall shed's un-named Patriot 4-6-0 No. 45517 in charge. *Peter Cookson.*

The Sheffield line through Pontefract Baghill - the Swinton & Knottingley - traditionally carried the bulk of what were termed North East-South West trains running between varying origins and destinations. On weekdays in summer, 1950 and 1955 11 northbound and 9 southbound expresses used the S&K. By summer, 1957 the number had increased to 13 northbound and 15 southbound; by 1968 it was back to 12 northbound and 10 southbound. The main trains were the Newcastle-Bristols which varied over the years between two, three and four in either direction. They were supplemented at various times by Bristol-York, Swansea-York, Birmingham-Newcastle, Cardiff - Newcastle and Worcester-York trains. The odd express also ran between York and Sheffield, varying between Midland and Victoria depending on the year. Probably the line's most prolific train was the Newcastle/York-Bournemouth, frequently formed of Southern Region green coaches. Another working worthy of note was the 7.5pm Newcastle to Bristol mail which called at Pontefract at 10.9pm to collect mail off the 9.46 arrival from Hull. The corresponding northbound train was the 7.20pm Bristol-Newcastle but it ran non-stop from Sheffield to York and the stock of the Hull connection returned empty to Selby.

The early hours of a summer Saturday in 1955 also saw the passage of the 9.45pm and 10.5pm Marylebone-Edinburgh trains - the so-called Starlight Specials - and their corresponding southbound workings. The S&K also carried timetabled troop trains - in summer 1955 they were the 12.25am Monday Only Sheffield Midland and 10.20pm Sunday Birmingham to Catterick Camp. Three or four Sheffield-York stopping trains a day served the smaller stations. A handful of overnight parcels trains also used the S&K.

The line's pivotal position on an inter-regional route led to a wonderous variety of motive power, ranging from ex-LMS Royal Scots, Jubilees and Patriots and LNER V2 2-6-2s, B16 4-6-0s and K3 2-6-0s to 4-4-0s of Midland, Great Central and LNER origin.

As the 1960s passed, the S&K was hit more and more by mining subsidence and it is fair to say that by the 1970s it was probably the worst affected main line in the country. In some places it was possible to look down the line and see a train appear, apparently out of the ground as it rose up from a sunken hollow. Although the National Coal Board paid for remedial work arising from subsidence, maintaining any kind of a worthwhile line speed became impossible and in 1973 BR switched all its North East-South West expresses to the Normanton route which was not so badly affected. During the 1970s and into the 1980s, seven or eight expresses each way travelled non-stop between York and Sheffield via Castleford, Normanton and Cudworth. Besides Bristol and Cardiff-Newcastle trains, they included Poole-Newcastle and Plymouth-Edinburgh services with an extra couple of trains each way on Fridays.

Although this robbed the S&K of virtually all its expresses, the local York-Sheffield service was considerably enhanced. In summer, 1978 it stood at eight trains each way, two going through to Scarborough. Just one express remained, the Fridays Only 19.33 York-Birmingham which ran to Penzance during the summer. But the local service was gradually whittled down - just five trains each way plus a summer season Sheffield-Scarborough in 1984 while in 2002 Pontefract Baghill clings to a rather sad remnant of just three northbound trains and two southbound, reduced to two each way on Saturdays.

With the introduction of High Speed Trains in 1981, resignalling and 115mph running were proposed under a £10.4 million upgrade for the whole North East-South West route, including the York-Normanton section, but the plan was short-lived. New BR InterCity management, faced with coach competition, economic recession and a serious embankment slip south of Normanton, rerouted their cross-country trains away from the Castleford line in May, 1984. Many were rerouted via the East Coast main line and Doncaster, others via Leeds, Moorthorpe and the southern end of the S&K.

The Castleford-Burton Salmon section was again left with only its summer seaside excursions - the summer Saturday Leicester-Scarborough was the last passenger train to travel between Sheffield and York this way until it was rerouted via the S&K from 1987. Passenger trains between Castleford and Burton Salmon were completely eliminated at the end of the 1992 summer season with the last run of the Sunday Only Wakefield-Scarborough, the return working of which also seems to have been the last train to use Castleford's Up platform. Or so we thought.

During December 2000 and January 2001, major engineering work at Leeds saw TransPennine trains diverted via Burton Salmon, Wakefield Kirkgate and Huddersfield, quite a few calling at Castleford where the Up platform was reopened for the duration. Occasionally, when the direct line between York and Leeds is blocked, passenger trains are diverted via Castleford and Methley, once again following the original route between the two cities.

Connecting the two main lines with Leeds was the NER's all stations service between Leeds City, Garforth, Kippax, Ledston and Castleford. Back in 1910 the weekdays only service consisted of five trains each way of which four ran to and from Pontefract Monkhill and Baghill. Extra trains ran between Leeds and Castleford on Tuesdays and Saturdays. By 1946 the slightly reduced service ran only between Leeds and Castleford with no extra Tuesday trains but an extra station, Bowers Halt, had been added between Kippax and Ledston. The 14-mile journey took between 37 and 43 minutes. By summer, 1950 only the 8.6am SX and 6.15pm Leeds-Castleford and 7am SX(6.55SO) and 4.50pm SX Castleford-Leeds

trains remained. Within months they were gone.

Before the Kippax branch service was withdrawn, Castleford was served by push-pull trains from both Leeds stations, of totally different lineages and approaching from opposite directions. From the Garforth end came the NER G5 0-4-4T and its two-coach train, while from the south approached an ex-GNR N1 0-6-2T with its push-pull formation from Leeds Central via the Methley Joint line. The Leeds Central service was much more frequent, faster and outlived the Garforth route. The summer 1950 timetable shows 11 weekday trains each way with extras on Saturdays and a Castleford-Leeds journey time of just over half an hour. Trains ran from early in the morning until late evening. In addition there were two morning trains from Wakefield Kirkgate via Westgate to Castleford and one back from Castleford. The same number of Leeds Central trains ran in summer, 1955, seven Leeds-bound and five Castleford-bound trains being push-pull, the rest conventionally hauled. However, only one Wakefield train remained, the 6.30am from Westgate. Three years later, diesel multiple units replaced steam and the service was

A late 1950s reminder of the S&K's most prolific train and the forerunner of today's Cross-Country services. Class V2 2-6-2 No. 60964 *The Durham Light Infantry* from 52A Gateshead shed approaches Pontefract Baghill from the north with what appears to be the Newcastle/York-Bournemouth express. Back in the 1950s BR followed the continental practice of giving most passenger trains a service number and this one is train 894. In 2002 Virgin Trains again uses this system for its Cross-Country and West Coast services. In the distance, a DMU is about to cross the viaduct on the line up to Pontefract Monkhill. *Peter Cookson*

Castleford Central once saw push-pull trains of Great Northern and North Eastern origin arrive from opposite directions. In this 2nd August, 1949 view, ex-NER G5 0-4-4T No. 67319 has arrived at the Up platform with the 6.15pm from Leeds City via Garforth while in the Down platform on the left, the 6.20pm from Leeds Central via the Methley Joint has arrived with ex-GNR Class N1 0-6-2T No. 9461 at the far end, still carrying its LNER number 20 months after nationalization. *John Edgington*

better than ever with 22 Leeds-bound trains and 20 from Leeds, plus the remaining 6.30am from Wakefield.

Castleford had one other service, this time from Cutsyke station on the L&Y Methley-Pontefract line which was served by Leeds City-Knottingley-Goole trains. In summer, 1957 the service stood at five trains from Leeds to Knottingley and six return, plus one Leeds to Goole and two from Goole to Leeds. By summer, 1968, the service consisted of five Leeds-Goole DMUs each way plus an 07.00 Knottingley-Leeds.

At Pontefract Monkhill, these trains supplemented those on the Wakefield-Goole line which also served the town's third station, Tanshelf. The Goole line's premier trains in the 1950s were the Hull-Wakefield expresses, in summer 1957 the 6.35pm from Hull(to Liverpool Exchange on Fridays) and 11.48am from Wakefield. Both trains were non-stop between Goole and Wakefield save for a Saturday stop at Snaith by the eastbound train. The westbound train was especially tightly timed, being allowed just 35 minutes for the 27.25 miles from Goole to Wakefield Kirkgate. Five other trains ran from

Wakefield to Goole and six from Goole to Wakefield plus one from Barnsley Exchange to Goole, one from Mirfield to Goole and one each from Goole and Knottingley to Bradford Exchange via Wakefield.

Having lost its East Coast main line status by 1871, the Knottingley-Askern line carried mainly local trains between Leeds or Wakefield, Knottingley and Doncaster, introduced by the L&Y to compensate for the GN's King's Cross-Leeds trains being switched to the new direct Doncaster-Leeds line in 1866. But it did continue to see some expresses and some interesting workings at that. Back in 1910, the L&Y ran eight all stations trains from Knottingley to Doncaster and seven back on weekdays with two each way on Sundays while its Liverpool-Harwich boat train ran this way until the first world war. The boat train actually called at Askern, the Harwich-bound train at 4.26pm and the Liverpool-bound train, which left Doncaster at 11.57am, upon request. From 1902, the GN ran three King's Cross-Harrogate expresses each way via Askern, Knottingley, Church Fenton and Wetherby. The Harrogate Pullman went the same route in the

The crack trains on the Wakefield-Goole line through Pontefract Monkhill and Knottingley in the 1950s were the 11.48am Wakefield to Hull and 6.35pm Hull to Wakefield expresses which ran non-stop between Goole and Wakefield. With immaculate Fowler Class 4P 2-6-4T No. 42311 in charge, the 6.35 from Hull rattles through Pontefract Monkhill during 1957. *Peter Cookson*

1920s and the York portion of the North Country Continental Harwich boat train also ran via Knottingley until the second world war. Normal passenger trains were withdrawn in September, 1948 but even in summer, 1955 the line still saw four booked passenger trains. These were the unadvertised Monday-Friday 6.43am Doncaster to Thorp Arch express, which called at Knottingley at 7.11, and the 5.28pm return, calling Knottingley at 6.21, the summer Saturday 8.44am Gorleston-on-Sea to York, through Knottingley at 3.45pm, and the summer Saturday 10am Lowestoft-Newcastle, pass Knottingley at 4.13pm. In addition, the line was regularly used by diverted East Coast expresses during engineering work between York and Doncaster.

On summer Saturdays during the 1950s and early 1960s the railway system in this part of the country was inundated with scores of extra trains carrying holidaymakers to and from the Yorkshire coast. They came from all parts of the West Riding, Lancashire, the East and West Midlands and even further afield. Funnelling through Burton Salmon , they travelled via either

York or Selby on their way to and from Scarborough, Bridlington or Butlin's holiday camp near Filey. Saturdays also saw extra relief trains, charter excursions and the like. Many trains utilised spare locomotives and coaching stock stored throughout the winter, and goods engines were pressed into service to meet this seasonal peak in demand. Such trains were too numerous to mention individually, but some of the more memorable ones through Castleford in 1957 included the 8.59am Bradford Exchange-Bridlington and 2.20pm return which normally used a pilot engine on the steeply graded lines between Castleford and Bradford, and the 9.5am from Liverpool Exchange to Scarborough Londesborough Road. In the same summer, the S&K saw 14 northbound and 10 southbound summer Saturday trains which included a number between Sheffield and the coast as well as the 8.25am Leicester London Road to Scarborough Central, the 9.57am Gloucester Eastgate to Filey Holiday Camp, the 11.50am Scarborough Londesborough Road to Leicester Central and two northbound trains from Newquay. Sundays and Bank Holidays also saw seaside trains of course, while these days were also popular choices for trains chartered by miners' welfare and social clubs in the locality. Special trains also ran for Pontefract races, using Tanshelf station which was the nearest to the racecourse.

In the later 1960s, increased car ownership, overseas package holidays, line closures and a drive to eliminate spare coaching stock saw a rapid decline in summer seasonal trains which continued through the 1970s and 1980s. A Leicester-Scarborough still ran each way over the S&K in 1991 but by the mid-1990s such trains had as good as disappeared. Among the last summer Saturday extras were just one train from Sheffield to Filey and a curious Sheffield to Hull via Scarborough train.

Freight traffic

The main driving force for freight traffic in the Castleford and Pontefract area was undoubtably coal with the railways once serving something like 15 pits in the immediate area alone. But there was also heavy long-distance traffic passing through between the Midlands and the North, between North and South, and between the far side of the Pennines, the West Riding and the North East.

Through traffic included the slower East Coast main line trains(usually loose-coupled or only partially fitted with continuous train brakes) that were routed via Askern, Knottingley, Burton Salmon and York to keep them clear of the faster traffic. The winter 1959/60 working timetable listed 14 Down or northbound trains between Shaftholme Junction and Knottingley but only five Up or southbound each 24 hours, although coal trains also ran that were not shown in the WTT. Those that were shown amounted mainly to loaded trains from Bentley Colliery(Doncaster) to Crofton Hall sidings(near Wakefield) and from Askern Colliery to Goole Docks for shipping, with empties coming the

Trains from Liverpool Exchange to Scarborough were among the many extras which made their way to the Yorkshire coast on summer Saturdays in the 1950s and early 1960s. Bank Hall Jubilee No. 45719 *Glorious* **pours a trail of smoke over the platform as it pounds through Pontefract Tanshelf with one such train. This train ran via Castleford and Selby until 1959 and via Pontefract and Goole from 1960.** *Peter Cookson*

other way. The 1.38pm Bentley to Crofton Hall class J was booked to take water at Norton. The line's only fully fitted express freight was the 9.20am MX Niddrie (1.45pm MO Heaton) to Doncaster Decoy class C which passed Knottingley at 5.6pm. At the other end of the scale, the local pick-up was train 26W running untimed from Doncaster to Knottingley. It called at Askern, Askern Colliery and Norton to attach wagons when required, and Cridling Stubbs Siding when required. The return working to Askern Colliery was booked to depart Knottingley at 2.10pm, calling at Cridling Stubbs Siding and Womersley, and at Norton when required.

The L&Y line from Goole to Knottingley, Pontefract and Wakefield or Methley saw between 25 and 30 booked freights each way per 24 hours. Much of the traffic was coal from various collieries to Goole for shipping, or to the yards at Crofton, Wakefield, Normanton and Healey Mills with corresponding returning empties. In the midst of all these slow moving mineral trains ran a number of express freights: the 9pm Hull to Aintree Class D, the 5pm Goole Sidings to Hunslet class D, the 10.55pm Manchester Brewery Sidings to Goole Beverley Sidings class D, the 10.30pm Bradford to Hull class E, 7.55pm Aintree to Hull class E, the 11.20pm Hull to Bradford Adolphus Street class E, and the 10.15pm Healey Mills-Hull class E. Local class K trips included the 6.5am Goole Sidings to Knottingley which as well as shunting intermediate stations called at Heck Ings level crossing to set down water cans and at Blackburn Lane to pick up water cans, and the 11am Knottingley to Goole Beverley Sidings which called at Blackburn Lane to drop off the refilled cans. Other trips were the 10.21am Pontefract Monkhill to Knottingley and 11.10am Knottingley to Wakefield Turners Lane which

Staple traffic for the Lancashire & Yorkshire line around Knottingley in August,1966 as in 2002 was coal. WD 2-8-0 No. 90030 from 50D Goole heads a westbound loaded coal train through Knottingley, or Knottingley(for Ferrybridge) as it was known then. Track remodelling was under way, the station had been stripped of its trainshed roof and before long the buildings and everything else will have given way to just two short platforms with bus shelters - but the coal traffic rumbles on. *Peter Cookson / N. E. Stead collection*

called at Featherstone when required, Ackton Hall Siding, Snydale Siding and Sharlston when required; and the 6pm Wakefield Whithams Sidings to Goole which called at Sharlston, Snydale Siding, Ackton Hall Siding, Pontefract Monkhill and Knottingley. In addition to these, the 1.35pm Goole to Turners Lane class H shunted at Snaith when required while looped to let other trains pass, as well as at Knottingley and Pontefract.

With around two dozen booked freights each way per 24 hours in winter 1959/60, S&K traffic was varied and fascinating. Most memorable were the vast trains carrying huge quantities of East Midlands iron ore from such places as Storefield and Wellingborough to the North East blast furnaces, hauled as far as York by ex-LMS Beyer-Garratts, Great Central 2-8-0s and BR 9F 2-10-0s - often so grimy it was impossible to read their numbers.

A considerable number of mixed freights ran between York and such places as Annesley, Mottram and Woodford Halse on the former Great Central system. Among noteworthy trains were three officially named class C expresses. These were the 6.40pm Park Lane(Gateshead) to Washwood Heath "The Birmingham Braked" (pass Pontefract 12.26am), the 5.30am York Dringhouses to Cardiff "The Welshman"(pass Pontefract 6.26) and the 5.55am York Dringhouses to Bristol "The Bristol" (pass Pontefract 6.53.) An eagerly awaited train was the Tuesdays and Thursdays 2.15pm class C empty Guinness tanks from Newcastle New Bridge Street to the brewery at Park Royal, London, which passed through Pontefract at 7.57pm. The northbound loaded train, the Mondays and Fridays 3.50pm Park Royal to Argyll Street passed through Baghill at 11.24pm. Two other overnight beer trains were the 6.10pm SX Burton-on-Trent to York Yard and the 9.10pm Monday Only Burton to Niddrie. Of other trains, the 9.15pm York to Birmingham fish called at Pontefract Baghill(10.28-38) to attach wagons when required.

As well as coal trains, the steady procession of freight between Burton Salmon, Castleford and Whitwood amounted to 40 Down(northbound) class C to H trains and 30 Up(southbound) classC to H trains per 24 hours in winter 1959/60. They included trains from the yards at Healey Mills, Wakefield, Ardsley and Normanton to York, Hull and the North East and trains from York, Hull and the North East to Normanton, Ardsley and Mirfield as well as trains to and from a variety of places across the Pennines, including Manchester, Liverpool, Birkenhead and Shrewsbury. Notable express workings along this route were the 7.30pm Liverpool Huskisson to Dringhouses, the 1.10am Monday excepted Dringhouses to Walton, the 5pm Sundays excepted Holyhead to York cattle train, and the 8.50pm Hull to Normanton fish - booked to detach wagons at Castleford 10.38-51pm, a train which also ran on Saturday evenings albeit an hour earlier. Catering for local traffic were the 6.35am Ardsley to Selby class H, booked to shunt at Castleford from 7.59 to 8.15, the 10.38am Selby to Ardsley class H, booked to shunt Castleford 11.20-11.40; the 6.30pm Normanton-Selby class H, the 8.50pm(9.5 on Sats) Selby-Normanton class E; the 6.15am Ardsley-Castleford class H which returned to Ardsley engine and brake van; and the 5pm Saturdays Ardsley-Castleford class H(6.4pm light engine on Monday to Friday), returning as the 7.10pm(6.45 Sats) Castleford to Wakefield Wrenthorpe yard. The 2.10pm Ardsley to York class H also called at Castleford from 3.13 to 3.28pm to detach.

Coal was collected from most local collieries by a series of trip workings from Gascoigne Wood marshalling yard near Selby until it closed in 1959. Worked by Selby engines, mostly Q6 0-8-0s, they ran along the Brackenhill Railway to Hemsworth Colliery, and via Fryston, Wheldale, and Prince of Wales collieries to Pontefract, Featherstone and Sharlston.

During the 1960s a new pattern of coal working was introduced to serve the big three new power stations at Ferrybridge, Eggborough and Drax. Merry-go-round block trains of 1,000 tons which discharged their loads without even stopping, started carrying the coal from pits modernised with new rapid loading bunkers. These replaced traditional colliery rail systems and gradually wiped out the use of NCB locomotives. In 1973, 10 collieries still used standard gauge locomotives but by the mid-1990s Selby was the nearest and only remaining deep mine to use a standard gauge loco - for shunting the sidings where a small amount of domestic coal was loaded. Knottingley was made the hub of these new coal operations, a diesel locomotive depot and wagon repair shop opening there in 1966. A special fleet

The most exciting of all the heavy freight trains which plied the S&K line had to be the mineral workings from the East Midlands to the North East headed by the LMS 2-6-6-2 Beyer Garratts. No. 47984 heads a heavy northbound coke train away from Pontefract Baghill in 1956. Within a few years the Garratts had been replaced by 9F 2-10-0s. *Peter Cookson*

of Class 47 locomotives equipped to run through the power station discharge hoppers at half a mile an hour was allocated there. In one week during the early 1970s the depot's 13 Class 47s succeeded in moving 440,000 tons of coal. As the power stations reached their peak demand following the completion of Drax B, Knottingley depot would be required to run up to 82 trains every 24 hours

The new Selby coalfield with its huge rail loading point at Gascoigne Wood added fresh impetus to coal workings as the rest of the coalfield declined. In 1989 Gascoigne Wood was despatching 95 loaded MGR trains a week to the Aire Valley power stations.

In 1980 the 47s were replaced by more powerful Class 56s. As British Rail was being privatised in the 1990s, the major power generating company National Power bought its own fleet of blue-liveried Class 59s and bogie hopper wagons, and set up its own traction depot on the site of the old traditional power station at Ferrybridge. The operation has since been taken over by English Welsh & Scottish Railway.

Most other forms of freight declined sharply from the 1960s onwards, either given up to road transport or a victim of Britain's continuing industrial decline. With the demise of coal shipping, the Knottingley-Goole line was especially hard hit and by 1973 the once bustling Hensall Junction-Goole section had no booked freight traffic and was ultimately reduced to single track.

Collieries were closing too - the whole Primrose Hill complex had gone by early 1970. Then as Margaret Thatcher's 1980s government set about its cynical destruction of Britain's coal industry, the region's pits fell one after the other, leaving Prince of Wales and Kellingley(Knottingley) the only deep mines in the Castleford and Pontefract area. At the end of January, 2002 the closure of Prince of Wales was announced leaving just the one pit at Kellingley. In July, U.K. Coal announced that even the big Selby Colliery complex, just 20 years old, would close by 2004 meaning a major upheaval in the power station coal workings as supplies would have to be brought from further afield.

But new freight traffic was won. A scheme to reduce sulphur dioxide emissions from Drax power station has resulted in major new freight traffic for the area. The power station requires a daily trainload of limestone from the Buxton area and sends out around 900,000 tonnes of gypsum a year with 12 trains a week going to a plaster works on the Settle and Carlisle line. In 2002 these were among the few freight trains still using the once-busy line through Featherstone.

All change

The rail system around Pontefract and Castleford suffered few cutbacks until after the second world war but one minor closure took place in 1869 when the Methley end of the Whitwood-Methley curve was closed to passenger traffic following the rerouting of York-Leeds trains via the new direct line. The curve remained open for goods traffic until 1929 when the Methley end was severed from the Leeds-Derby line, the rest remaining open to provide a connection with the Methley Joint.

One more cutback came in 1926 when the LNER cut the Leeds City-Pontefract Baghill service back to Castleford, closing the Castleford-Cutsyke Junction and Pontefract Monkhill-Baghill curves to regular passenger traffic.

The first major blow in a general process of decline, which ultimately led to the railway network remaining today, came in 1947. On 10th March, the LMS closed all intermediate stations between Knottingley and Shaftholme Junction and withdrew the Knottingley-Doncaster portion of its Leeds-Knottingley-Doncaster stopping service. The rerouting of remaining expresses from 27th September, 1948 completed the withdrawal of daily public passenger trains from the Askern branch. Nationalization in 1948 did nothing to halt the creeping tide of rationalization and the Leeds City-Castleford passenger service via Garforth and Kippax was next to go on 22nd January, 1951.

On 5th May, 1958 the Castleford-Cutsyke Junction curve was reopened to passenger traffic and the Leeds Central-Castleford service, now operated by diesel multiple units, was intensified and extended to Pontefract Monkhill with a reversal at Castleford. On 4th January, 1960 the service was further extended to Pontefract Baghill, bringing regular passenger trains back to the Monkhill-Baghill line.

The 1960s brought a wave of closures and the Brackenhill Light Railway was the first to go on 1st January, 1962. Then came the Beeching years when lines and stations were closed one after the

In the spring of 1958, diesel multiple units replaced steam on a number of Pontefract and Castleford area services. Perceived as clean and modern, they were popular with passengers and brought new hope for the future of local services. On 3rd March, the first day of Wakefield-Goole diesel services, a brand new three-car Metropolitan-Cammell set leaves Pontefract Monkhill with a Goole to Bradford working while a Derby Lightweight unit forms a service to Leeds Central. The DMUs were the mainstay of Yorkshire's surviving local train network for the next 30 years. *Peter Cookson*

other and surviving services modified. The first blow came in 1963 when local goods services were withdrawn from the Garforth-Castleford line, leaving only colliery traffic and occasional use as a diversionary route. The Leeds Central-Castleford-Pontefract Baghill service was withdrawn in November, 1964, leaving the Cutsyke curve freight only yet again.

The most significant closure came on 2nd January, 1967 when BR withdrew the Wakefield-Goole passenger service, including all passenger trains between Wakefield and Pontefract Monkhill, and closed Featherstone and Pontefract Tanshelf stations. To compensate, the Leeds-Knottingley service was increased and extended to Goole while track and signalling between Wakefield, Knottingley and Hensall Junction was upgraded ready for heavy merry-go-round coal trains serving the new power stations. It is often claimed that the passenger service on this line was sacrificed to provide capacity for power station coal traffic. The Whitwood-Methley curve, having lost all its remaining passenger traffic upon withdrawal of the Castleford Central-Leeds Central service in 1964, closed altogether on 27th March, 1967 when freight trains ceased running between the Methley Joint and Whitwood. However, this complete closure merely allowed work to proceed on reinstating the original connection with the Midland line ready to serve a big new marshalling yard at Stourton, near Leeds, the curve reopening to freight traffic on 31st July. The yard was never completed but on 7th October, 1968 Leeds-Goole passenger trains were rerouted via the curve and a reversal at Castleford Central. The Central-Cutsyke curve was a passenger line yet again but the Methley-Cutsyke Junction line was reduced to freight only and Cutsyke station closed.

Also in 1968, the southern end of the S&K saw an increase in passenger traffic when Leeds-Sheffield trains were rerouted via Wakefield and Moorthorpe because of mining subsidence on the Midland route through Normanton and Cudworth. The following year saw complete closure between Garforth and Allerton Main

The Castleford-Garforth line lost its regular passenger service in 1951 but continued to see special passenger traffic up to its closure as a through route in 1969. On 21st September, 1958 it was graced by a Railway Correspondence and Travel Society railtour with ex-Great Northern J6 0-6-0s 64268 and 64222. The special is seen passing Ledston station and Allerton Bywater Colliery while heading towards Castleford.
D. Butterfield / N. E. Stead collection

Methley Junction on 24th July, 1980. Having just left the Midland line, the 12.12 Leeds to Goole diesel multiple unit heads along Hudson's curve to Whitwood while the former L&Y line to Pontefract passes in front of the houses on the right. *Peter Rose*

Junction, ending the Garforth-Castleford line's status as a through route. The remaining portion continued to carry coal from local collieries and the Bowers Row opencast mine.

Generally, the post-Beeching years of the late 1960s and early 1970s presented a desolate scene with surviving local passenger services often sparse, running at inconvenient times and by roundabout routes. They were being deserted by commuters as car ownership grew while on the roads traffic congestion was making its debut. In 1972 BR tried to stem the loss with a major promotion of its local services in the West Riding, each route being given its own brand name, Leeds-Castleford-Pontefract-Goole being "The Goole Line." The campaign worked and an annual five per cent loss in passengers was turned into a five per cent gain.

Then on 1st January, 1976 the West Yorkshire County Council, through its Passenger Transport Executive, took financial responsibility for the county's public transport with the aim of securing the future of those local rail services that remained. At first it only supported the Leeds-Micklefield service but since 1978 when its responsibilities were cemented by the signing of a £4.2 million financial support contract with BR, the PTE has

led an amazing revival of local train travel through competitive fares, imaginative multi-journey tickets, more attractive timetables, refurbished stations, new trains and even reopened lines. The Leeds-Castleford-Knottingley and Leeds-Wakefield-Moorthorpe services were among those to be secured. In May, 1988 a direct service between Castleford and Wakefield was reinstated and Castleford-Leeds services intensified when Leeds-Barnsley-Sheffield trains were rerouted via a reversal at Castleford.

Outside West Yorkshire, however, things were not so rosy. Trains between Knottingley and Goole were steadily eroded until only two from Leeds and three from Goole remained in 2002. The passenger service over the northern section of the S&K was little better, the PTE refusing to support the Pontefract Baghill-Moorthorpe section even though it fell within West Yorkshire.

The government's pit closure programme of the 1980s and early 1990s led to the abandonment of several remaining freight lines in the Castleford and Pontefract area. First to go, abandoned in 1982, was the Pontefract-Methley line and the surviving portion of the Methley Joint which had been retained to serve Newmarket Colliery. In 1989, coal trains ceased running from Bowers Row

The official opening of the new Pontefract Tanshelf station and reopening of the Wakefield-Pontefract Monkhill line to passenger services on 12th May, 1992.
Step off the train here and as you walk from the station your nostrils will delight to the sweet smell of liquorice from Pontefract's remaining couple of factories. *Steve Chapman*

and the Castleford-Garforth line was cut back to Allerton Bywater Colliery. The colliery closed in March, 1992, ending coal traffic altogether but trains bringing spoil from Selby mine for tipping at Ledston kept the line in business another four years. It was officially taken out of use in 1997 during resignalling of the Castleford area. The track to Ledston remained, disused, in 2001. Most of the Castleford-Garforth trackbed still survived in 2001, and with sizeable communities around Kippax and Swillington plus mounting traffic congestion in Leeds, this old route really needs reopening in whole or part for commuters.

In some quarters, the loss of coal traffic heralded new opportunities for the passenger railway. The closure of Sharlston and Ackton Hall (Featherstone) collieries, together with the near elimination of power station coal traffic on the Wakefield-Pontefract line, allowed the events of 1967 to be reversed and the line reopened for passengers. On 11th May, 1992, thanks to funding from Europe and the West Yorkshire Passenger Transport Authority(which succeded the county

council in 1985), a new Wakefield-Pontefract-Knottingley passenger service was launched under a £1.1 million scheme which included re-signalling and new stations at Streethouse(near Sharlston), Featherstone and Tanshelf. Since then,it has again been just about possible to travel by train between Wakefield and Goole by changing at Pontefract Monkhill or Knottingley.

Yet as the privatised railway industry talked of incorporating the S&K in a new East Coast trunk freight route, things reached an all-time low on 29th October, 2001. The Wakefield-Goole line east of Hensall Junction became effectively disused while Pontefract incredibly found itself with no passenger trains at all on Saturdays and only S&K trains on weekdays. From that day, the train operator Arriva replaced all Leeds-Goole, Castleford-Knottingley, Wakefield-Pontefract Monkhill, and S&K Saturday trains with buses because it was short of train drivers. The Wakefield-Pontefract and Castleford-Knottingley trains were reinstated on 25th February, 2002 and the Goole service in June.

Our thanks are due to the following for their valuable assistance: Robert Anderson, John Beaumont, Ron Hollier, David Holmes, Industrial Railway Society, North Eastern Railway Association, Pontefract Reference Library, Pontefract Museum, Tony Ross.

METHLEY-CASTLEFORD-BURTON SALMON

Above: B1 4-6-0 No. 61297 of 56B Ardsley shed hauls a load of coal from Prince of Wales Colliery, Pontefract, along the Methley Joint line past Methley South to the marshalling yards at Ardsley on 10th May, 1961. The splitting signals in front of the signal box control the junction between the lines to Lofthouse Junction, Cutsyke and Pontefract(left) and down towards Whitwood Junction(right.)
Peter Cookson / Neville Stead collection

Below: A Derby Works lightweight DMU takes the Whitwood line at Methley South while on its way from Leeds Central to Castleford with a 1950s Methley Joint service. *Peter Cookson*

Two views of the vee-shaped Methley South station in September, 1958.
Above: Looking east with the line down to Lofthouse Junction and the L&Y Methley-Pontefract line on the left and the curve to Whitwood on the right. Although well kept, it is said the platforms on the left were never used by regular passenger trains. *Peter Cookson*

Below: Looking west from the Castleford-bound platform *Peter Cookson/N. E. Stead collection.*

Above: A two-car Derby Works DMU in late 1970s refurbished livery forming the 12.58 Goole to Leeds passes the North Eastern Railway pattern signal box at Whitwood Junction while taking the curve towards Methley on 24th July, 1980. The overbridge carries the Methley-Pontefract line. The box closed during the Castleford area resignalling in 1997 but still stood in 2002. *Peter Rose*

Below: A reminder that not too many years ago, coal wasn't Castleford's only local freight traffic. Seen from the Methley-Pontefract line on 24th July, 1980, diesel shunter 08311 working trip 9K44 conveying an empty hopper wagon from the local glassworks back to Healey Mills, prepares to drop off stores at Whitwood signal box. The Whitwood Mere branch went off left just beyond the road bridge. *Peter Rose*

The 1969 BR Sectional Appendix shows the 6 miles 1348yds from Altofts to Burton Salmon as having signal boxes at Whitwood Jn. (1 mile 1017yds from Altofts Jn.), Castleford Gates (1359yds from Whitwood Jn.), Castleford Station (506yds), Old Station(865yds), Fryston(1 mile 779yds) and Burton Salmon(2 miles 312yds.)

One extra running line was the Down Goods from Castleford Gates to Station.

Signalling was Absolute Block with No Block on the Down Goods.

Maximum speed on main lines was 60mph.

An Up refuge siding connected to the Garforth branch at Old Station could take 59 wagons, engine and brake van, and a Down goods loop at Fryston 70 wagons, engine and brake.

Signal boxes abolished since September, 1957 were Wheldale and Fryston North with Fryston South becoming Fryston.

Under signalling alterations listed in an Appendix supplement dated 8th February, 1975, Old Station box was reduced to Castleford East Branch ground frame controlled by Station box.

WHITWOOD BRANCH: The normal position of Pottery Street level crossing gates is across the line, and drivers, when approaching, must sound the locomotive whistle to inform the person appointed for the duty that the level crossing gates require to be reversed. *BR Eastern Region Sectional Appendix, 1969.*

The Whitwood branch was deleted from the Appendix by an amendment dated 8.2.75.

Above: The former North Eastern branch to Whitwood Mere served the Laporte chemical works and was known locally as the Potteries Branch because of the potteries along its 505-yard route.
Here, one of the ex-NER J72 0-6-0Ts allocated to Normanton shed for working Castleford area trips, No. 68726, approaches Pottery Street level crossing in about 1960 with a train of tank wagons for the works. Behind it is Clokie & Co.'s pottery. *Peter Cookson*

Below: At the branch terminus with the Laporte plant behind it, 68726 starts to run round its train before propelling the wagons into the works sidings. *Peter Cookson*

David Holmes was Castleford station master for two years until February, 1970 when station masters gave way to area managers. Some years before, Cutsyke and Kippax had their own station masters.

"On paper we had 55 staff but less in practice. Besides assistant SM John Smith and myself, there were two booking clerks, a goods office clerk, a staff clerk, signalmen, relief signalmen, two porters at each station, two shunters and a travelling checker. We had a checker at Glasshoughton due to incoming coal for the coke works. On 18th November, 1968 the goods office in Castleford yard closed and the work transferred to an office on the platform.

"Traffic was over 90 per cent freight. In the late 1960s, Class 37s covered most local duties while single York Class 20s took coal from Wheldale to Glasshoughton coke works. Much of the output from Bowers opencast was hauled to Goole docks by Goole 37s. Trains from Newmarket Colliery, mainly bound for Skelton Grange power station, Leeds, reversed at Glasshoughton and most of the Glasshoughton output had to reverse at Pontefract Monkhill.

"A Class 03 pilot shunted the goods yard and took raw materials to Lumb's glassworks next to Castleford Gates signal box. Sand came from Middleton Towers, lime from the Peak District and soda ash from Northwich. Lumb's had some ancient wagon turntables. Forwarded traffic, like the famous square whisky bottles, no longer went by rail but we did once send a large consignment of hurricane lamp glasses for Africa via Birkenhead docks. By then the goods yard was only used for shunting and wagons of coal spillage salvaged from marshalling yards. The pilot also went to the East branch. Known locally as the Ryebread branch because of traffic it once carried, it mainly served the Hickson & Welch chemical works. Some chemicals went to Germany and a local headmaster helped translate any German document-

ation we didn't understand.

"On 4th January, 1970, the York-Manchester passenger service finished. Many passengers travelled to York, especially for the races, and to Church Fenton for the air display. On summer weekends we were very busy with people going to the seaside. In June and July especially, as many as five guarenteed excursions ran each Sunday from Central, occasionally from Cutsyke. Mostly for working men's and miners' welfare clubs, they mainly went to Scarborough or Bridlington and a BG parcels van was marshalled in the middle of the train for refreshments and the beer. In 1968 we ran 20 such trains. The most farcical working was a long train from Cutsyke to Cleethorpes. The empty stock had to make two reversals and two more once loaded. At one stage, it was stuck at Glasshoughton as recent resignalling had made its next move impossible. The points had to be changed by crank handle and the train propelled facing road by its Class 40 loco over a busy level crossing before reaching the short platform. For the return working we had another Class 40 ready to couple on the rear and avoid the run-round manoeuvres. Even so, many passengers bailed out into the colliery sidings where they worked during the week, having had enough delays on the outward run.

"In 1969 we ran six specials to London when Castleford reached the Rugby League cup final, two to Wembley Central, two to St. Pancras and two to King's Cross. Same again in 1970.

"Reopening of the Whitwood curve in 1968 brought a Deltic roaring through Castleford about 10 o'clock each night on a Leeds-Edinburgh parcels but it didn't stop. Heavy parcels traffic had recently been switched to Wakefield. The move left a lot of old four-wheel barrows to get rid of so we stuck them in a wagon and labelled it to York Works!"

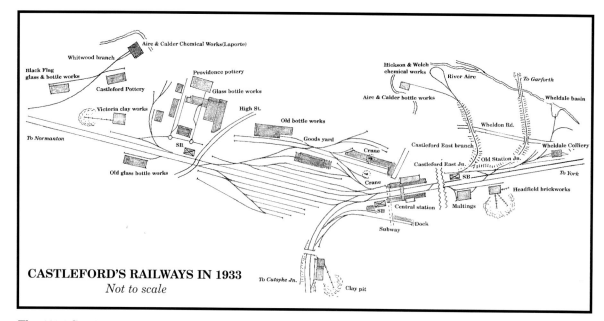

CASTLEFORD'S RAILWAYS IN 1933
Not to scale

The 1956 Stations Handbook shows Castleford Central goods yard as equipped with a 5-ton crane and able to handle general goods, furniture vans, carriages, motor cars, portable engines, machines on wheels, livestock, horse boxes and prize cattle vans. Central station could handle carriages and motor cars by passenger and parcels train for which a dock was provided at the south end on the east side of the main line. Castleford Central goods closed with effect from 5th January, 1970 after a spell as an unstaffed public delivery siding. A couple of sidings were retained for shunting movements but the rest of the track was lifted while the goods shed was rented out to local firms. The site has since been completely redeveloped.

Below: With Castleford goods yard and the Old Bottle Works on its right, begrimed Wakefield Jubilee 4-6-0 No. 45739 *Ulster* rolls a Wakefield-Scarborough excursion over the level crossing at Castleford Gates in about 1964. *Peter Cookson*

Above: The Castleford-Leeds Central service via the Methley Joint had been turned over to diesel multiple units by the time this late 1950s picture was taken but this train, the Saturday Only 2.11pm from Castleford was still a job for an N1 0-6-2T, in this case No. 69450 seen departing Castleford Central with goods yard activity on the right. *Both pictures on this page by Peter Cookson*

Below: Another begrimed Wakefield Jubilee on holiday traffic. No. 45589 *Gwalior* gets a Castleford to Blackpool excursion away from Central station and over the junction with the curve to Cutsyke and Pontefract in summer, 1964. The far end of the train is just passing Castleford Station signal box.

Above: At 1.55pm on 4th November, 1961, Fowler Class 4 2-6-4T No. 42411 of 56C Leeds Copley Hill shed pulls out of Castleford Central station and heads towards Castleford Gates with the 1.49pm to Leeds Central via the Methley Joint, a train which includes articulated coaches. The junction with the Cutsyke curve shows signs of recent renewal. *Both pictures on this page by Robert Anderson*

Left: Castleford was noted for its surviving twin semaphore splitting signals which controlled movements to the Pontefract and Normanton lines from both Up and Down lines, necessitated by the fact that all local passenger trains reversed at the Down platform.

In this late 1970s scene, the home signal controlling movements from the Down Normanton line to the Up Normanton is off for a Knottingley-Leeds Class 110 DMU. The other signals are, from left: Up Normanton to Pontefract, Up Normanton, and Down Normanton to Pontefract. The small shunt signal on the right controls movements into the severely rationalized goods yard. Castleford Station signal box was closed and the semaphores replaced with colour lights in 1997.

Above: The former NER Castleford station became Castleford Central in 1952 to distinguish it from the former L&Y station which became Castleford Cutsyke. It reverted to just Castleford in 1969 after Cutsyke had closed. This was Castleford Central looking south in the late 1950s. The only building remaining in 2002 is that nearest the camera on the right with the two chimney stacks. The main building fronted by the canopy was replaced by a large glass shelter. Beyond the then enclosed footbridge is the main goods yard.
Peter Cookson

Below: The date is 30th December, 2000 but already this event has become a railway memory. During a major phase of remodelling work at Leeds City station in December 2000/January, 2001, TransPennine services were diverted to run between York or Selby and Huddersfield via Castleford where a good few were booked to call for coach connections with Leeds. For this the disused Up platform had to be reopened. As the footbridge was not suitable for use, temporary access had to be made by knocking down part of the platform wall off the picture to the right to connect the platform with a subway. The wall was bricked up again when the trains reverted to their normal route. Virgin CrossCountry services were also diverted via Castleford, recalling the 1970s and early 1980s when they were booked to travel this way. The Up platform buildings which were just beyond the bridge, had only recently been demolished. *Steve Chapman*

Above: Two-way working of Castleford's platforms was in operation long before the advent of diesel multiple units as seen here. On 2nd August, 1949, N1 0-6-2T No. 9461, still sporting LNER number and livery, prepares to depart from the Down platform with the 7.30pm to Leeds Central. *John Edgington*

Castleford departures. Weekdays, 5th June - 24th September, 1950

am

6.37		All stations via Ardsley to Leeds Central
6.55	SO	All stations via Garforth to Leeds City
7.0	SX	All stations via Garforth to Leeds City
7.7		All stations via Ardsley to Leeds Central
7.29		All stations to York
7.37		Normanton. From York.
		To Blackpool North Sats 24/6-26/8
7.47		Stanley then all stations to Leeds Central
8.20		Stanley then all stations to Leeds Central
9.6		Scarborough via Monk Fryston & York
9.20		All stations via Ardsley to Leeds Central
10.31	SO	Bridlington *10/6-16/9 From Bradford*
10.48		Manchester Victoria via Normanton
		To Blackpool Cen on Sats 17/6-2/9.
11.2	SO	Scarborough via York
		From Bradford Ex. 10/6-16/9

pm

12.1		Sherburn SO & York *From Manchester V.*
12.18	SO	All stations via Ardsley to Leeds Central
1.9		Newcastle via York *From Liverpool Ex.*
		Not Sats 24/6-26/8
1.10		All stations via Ardsley to Leeds Central
1.22	SO	Stanley, Ardsley and Bradford Exchange
		From Scarborough. Not after Sept 16th
2.1	SO	York *From Manchester Victoria*

pm(*cont.*)

2.1	SO	All sations via Ardsley to Leeds Central
2.30		Liverpool Exchange via Normanton
2.44		All stations via Ardsley to Leeds Central
3.23	SO	Normanton *All stations from York*
3.56		All stations via Ardsley to Leeds Central
4.22	SO	Stanley, Ardsley and Bradford Exchange
		From Bridlington. Not after Sept. 16th
4.50	SX	All stations via Garforth to Leeds City
5.2	SO	All stations to Church Fenton then York
		From Blackpool North 24/6-26/8
5.8	SX	All stations via Ardsley to Leeds Central
5.21	SO	All stations via Ardsley to Leeds Central
5.52		Manchester Victoria via Normanton
6.10		All stations via Ardsley to Leeds Central
7.20		York *From Manchester Exchange*
7.30		All stations via Ardsley to Leeds Central
7.38		Liverpool Exchange via Normanton
		From Newcastle
9.22	FX	Normanton *From Scarborough*
9.32	FO	Normanton *From Scarborough*
9.47		Church Fenton & York *From Liverpool*
10.12	FSO	Stanley, Ardsley, Holbeck, Leeds Central
10.22	FSX	Stanley, Ardsley, Holbeck, Leeds Central
11.0	SO	Stanley, Ardsley, Holbeck, Leeds Central

In 1950 the return fare from Castleford to London was 48s 1d(£2.40)3rd class and 72s 2d(£3.61) 1st.

Above: Having just arrived with the Saturday Only 12.46pm from Leeds Central, N1 0-6-2T No. 69450 is prepared to run round its train for the return working. It is 3rd January, 1959 and by the end of the month 69450 will be in store along with the other six remaining members of its class. In spite of this, the loco is well groomed complete with builder's plate on the leading splasher. *John Beaumont*

Below: When new diesels introduced to the Methley Joint service in 1954 suffered teething troubles, steam locos and stock had to be drafted in from other parts of the country until the problems were sorted out. In this scene which oozes 1950s culture, the Leeds Central service at Castleford is formed of a Manchester London Road push & pull set while the locomotive on the rear is an N7 0-6-2T brought up from London's Great Eastern suburban lines. *C. Boulden*

Above: J72 0-6-0T No. 68701 ambles through the Up platform at Castleford with a local trip working in the late 1950s. *Peter Cookson*

SHORT MEMORIES

Summer, 1960: Royal Scot 4-6-0s see regular use on the 9.40am Sheffield-York and 1pm return locals. 46131 on 30th July and 46147 on 13th August.

5.8.60: 46131 heads the 7.48am Nottingham-Newcastle relief as far as York and returns with the 12.18pm Newcastle-Birmingham relief.

Easter, 1961: Some Leeds Central-Pontefract Baghill trains revert to steam because DMUs are needed to strengthen other services.

Above: A closer view of the Up side station buildings when still intact but largely unused on 14th June, 1994. They were demolished late in 2000. Castleford Central station dates from 1871 when it replaced the original station a little further north. *Steve Chapman*

A 1980s proposal to reroute Leeds-Castleford-Knottingley and Goole services via Normanton and Wakefield Westgate thankfully did not materialise. The Leeds-Castleford journey would have taken 31 minutes compared with 19 via Methley.

Above: The 10.30am express from Liverpool Exchange to Newcastle via Manchester Victoria, the Calder Valley and Wakefield Kirkgate calls at Castleford Central shortly after 1pm in 1958 with well maintained Jubilee No. 45717 *Dauntless* from 27A Liverpool Bank Hall shed in charge. *Peter Cookson*

Below: Black Five 4-6-0 No. 44929 of 26B Agecroft shed enters Castleford Central at 2.28pm on 4th November, 1961 with the 2.2pm York to Liverpool via the Calder Valley and Manchester Victoria. In the 21st century a typically fast journey between York and Castleford would take 51 minutes given a good connection at Leeds, compared with the 26 minutes of this steam age train. *Robert Anderson*

Above: J72 No. 68701 on local trip duty again, this time on 9th July, 1960 when it was making its way to the Whitwood branch after serving various other small branches and sidings north of Castleford station. Castleford Old Station Junction and the site of the original station are in the far distance, near the factory chimney. *D. P. Leckonby*

Castleford private sidings(excluding National Coal Board), 1956

Austin Bros., Castleford Central
Bellamy's Confectionary Works, Central
Clokie & Co.'s Siding, Whitwood Branch
Crowley Russell & Co., Central
T. Fawcett & Sons, Central
J. Hartley & Co., Headfield Brickworks,
Castleford Central
Hartley's(Castleford) Ltd., Victoria Brickworks,
Castleford Central
Hickson & Welch Ltd., Castleford East branch
Hickson's Timber Impregnation Co., East branch
Hunt Bros., Aire & Calder Chemical Works,
Whitwood branch
J. Lumb & Co., High Town Siding, Cental
J. Lumb & Co., New Works, Central
Neuweiler & Co., Castleford Central
North Eastern Gas Board, Whitwood Colliery
Whitwood Chemical Co., Whitwood Colliery
William Womersley, Loscoe Farm, Whitwood Coll.
Yorkshire Brick Co., Glasshoughton Colliery
Yorkshire Coking & Chemical Co.,
Glasshoughton Colliery

The Castleford East branch ran just 657 yards from Old Station Jn. to Hickson's chemical works. It was worked by One Engine in Steam regulations.

The 1969 BR Sectional Appendix gave the following instruction: On the Down journey the train must stop at Wheldale Road bridge until the driver receives a hand signal from the guard to proceed. The guard must report to Hickson's gate office on arrival and a man will be detailed to supervise the car park and road crossings to ensure that the gates leading to the firm's sidings are open for the train to enter the works. The guard will then give the hand signal to the driver and precede the train to see that the points are correctly set and the line is clear to the yard.

The train must be propelled in the Down direction... and only the Castleford diesel shunting engine must be used....speed on the branch must not exceed 4mph (a supplement dated 8th February, 1975 added that up to 6 wagons could be propelled.)

A similar instruction in the 1960 Appendix told the driver to await a hand signal from the crossing keeper and also stated that only classes J71 and J72 locos must be used and that they must always go down bunker first. The locomotive must be in front and the guard's van in the rear in both directions.

Above: Wheldale Colliery exchange sidings looking towards Castleford on 8th April, 1970. The York-Normanton main line and a brickworks are on the left and, in the distance, are Old Station Junction, and maltings which were served by their own siding into the 1970s. National Coal Board locomotives shunting the yard are 0-6-0STs, on the left, *Mexborough*, built by Hunslet in 1938, works No. 1902 and, right, *Bawtry*, built by Hunslet in 1932, works No.1698. *Robert Anderson*

CASTLEFORD(OLD STATION)-WORKING OF TRAINS TO AND FROM WHELDALE COLLIERY: Trains from the colliery must depart via No.1 or 2 sidings and trains entering the colliery must use the contractors siding. Before any train is propelled in the sidings towards the siding outlet, the guard must obtain the permission of the signalman at Castleford Old Station box by use of the telephone located at the exit from the sidings. *BR Eastern Region(Northern Area) Sectional Appendix, 1969. In a supplement to the appendix dated 8th February, 1975, this instruction was amended to read: the guard must obtain the permission of the signalman at Castleford Station box by use of the telephone located at the ground frame.*

Left: An example of the variety of active steam which could still be found around Castleford for several years after the end of steam on BR. Wheldale Colliery's 0-6-0ST No. S115 *Frank*, built by Hawthorn Leslie of Newcastle-Upon-Tyne in 1922 (works No. 3534) was in steam at 11.50am on 9th September, 1969. *David Holmes*

Above: *Bawtry,* looking resplendent in ex-works green livery and white lining while working Wheldale Colliery sidings on 8th April, 1970. *Robert Anderson*

Below: At the start of the NCB branch which crossed Wheldon Road and led to the staithes at Wheldale Basin, *Mexborough* blasts up the bank into Wheldale Colliery yard on the same day, having just brought a load of coal over the internal line from Fryston Colliery while deputising for a diesel which was under repair. *Robert Anderson*

Colliery Steam in the Castleford area 1969

Wheldale: Hawthorn Leslie 0-6-0ST *Frank*, and Hunslet 0-6-0STs *Bawtry* and *Mexborough*.
Fryston: Hunslet 0-6-0STs *Diana*(1441/23) on standby and *Coronation* (1810/37) out of use, Austerity 0-6-0ST No. 26 and Hudswell Clarke 0-6-0T *Fryston No.2*.
Glasshoughton: Hudswell Clarke 0-6-0Ts S103 (1864/52) and S118 (1870/53), and Hunslet 0-6-0ST GH No.4 (3855/54.)
Glasshoughton Coking Plant: Hawthorn Leslie 0-6-0ST 3575/23 and Hunslet Austerities 2868/43 and 2897/43 handled yard work while Stephenson & Hawthorn 0-6-0 fireless 8082/58 with cab on top powered the coke car.
Peckfield: Hunslet Austerity 0-6-0ST 1763/44 assisting Hudswell Clarke 0-6-0 diesel.
Primrose Hill: Hunslet 0-6-0STs *Jubilee* (1725/35), *Astley*, Austerities 3168/44, 3180/ 44 and 3836/55.
Bowers Row opencast: RSH Austerity 0-6-0ST 7164/44 the regular loco
Allerton Bywater workshops usually overhauling two steam locos at a time.

Above: An event to delight enthusiasts in 1981 was the return to steam at Wheldale Colliery of Hunslet-built Austerity 0-6-0ST No.7, works No. 3168 of 1944, which had been stored at Allerton Bywater Colliery and then overhauled at Allerton Bywater workshops before being used for trials with different grades of coal on behalf of the company which built it. No. 3168 went back to work in November taking coal to the canal staithes and to Fryston Colliery for washing, or spoil to the tip. The trials ended on 6th January, 1982 but a dire shortage of workable diesels kept 3168 in business, often in steam 24 hours a day, until 24th September, 1982 after which it passed into preservation.

Here, No. 3168 moves internal wagons along dubious track in the exchange sidings on 11th January, 1982. Behind it, a wagon is being loaded onto or off a lorry. The conical chimney denotes that 3168 is fitted with an underfeed stoker and the Hunslet gas producer system designed to cut black smoke. *Peter Rose*

Below: Steam had left Wheldale Colliery for good and there were only diesels to work the NCB rail system by the time this picture was taken on 8th February, 1986. Rail traffic, latterly only trains taking spoil for dumping on the site of Fryston Colliery, had ended by July, 1987 and the pit closed completely not long after. The front loco is Hunslet diesel hydraulic 0-6-0 No. 7276.
Like most pits, Wheldale also had a narrow gauge system and one of the locos can just be seen underneath the structure in the left distance. *Adrian Booth*

Above: About a mile north of Wheldale was neighbouring Fryston Colliery, another fascination with steam working which survived into the 1970s. On 21st June, 1969, Class 47 No. D1579 and a southbound special Freightliner pass Fryston signal box and the site of Fryston goods station which closed in 1960. Renamed from Wheldon Bridge in 1882, Fryston goods was equipped to handle mineral, coal, side to side wagonload traffic and livestock. *Adrian Booth*

Below: Classic Fryston. An old NER slotted signal prevents passage onto the York-Normanton main line as one of the robust Hudswell Clarke 0-6-0Ts once commonplace throughout the NCB's North Yorkshire Area, *Fryston No.2*(works No. 1883 of 1955) stands between the main line and the colliery engine shed with Austerity 0-6-0ST *Parkhill*(Robert Stephenson & Hawthorn 7291 of 1945) on 8th April, 1970. *Robert Anderson*

Above: A view which shows the extent of railway situated between the York-Normanton line and the river at Fryston Colliery. On 8th April, 1970 *Fryston No. 2* storms up the yard with a load of coal from the canal basin, passing a wagon tippler on the right. Fryston Colliery closed in December, 1985 and by April, 1987 all but the engine shed had been cleared. Until July, 1987 the site was used as a tip for spoil from Wheldale.

Below: At Fryston on the same day, Austerity 0-6-0ST No. 26 *Parkhill* was coupling up to her train of internal wagons when a snow storm suddenly swept across the river basin, blacking out the sun. Then, without a trace of a slip she barked up from the basin with these 22 hoppers in tow. *Both Robert Anderson*

Above: A fine panoramic view of Burton Salmon looking west, probably in the late 1940s, complete with NER slotted signals, the old signal box on the right, its larger replacement on the left and ancient coaching stock in use as engineers' vehicles parked in the cattle dock. The line from York to Castleford and Normanton goes straight ahead towards Fairburn Tunnel while the Knottingley branch curves to the left. In 2002 this key junction no longer existed, the Knottingley and Normanton lines running completely separate from Milford Junction to Burton Salmon where they just diverge. *Ernest Sanderson*

Below: A 1960s Rotherham Masbrough to York Dringhouses class D express freight which has travelled via the S&K comes off the Knottingley branch at Burton Salmon past a now trackless cattle dock hauled by Black Five 4-6-0 No. 44965.
The engine is from 2E Saltley shed(Birmingham) which regularly provided engines for freight work over this route. *Peter Cookson / N. E. Stead collection*

Above: With the goods yard on its left and the station on the its right, Q6 0-8-0 No. 63450 from 50C Selby shed trundles northwards along the YNM line through Burton Salmon with coal from the Castleford area to the marshalling yard at Gascoigne Wood on 3rd September, 1958. The passenger station closed in 1959.

Burton Salmon goods yard had no fixed crane but in 1956 was shown as able to handle general goods traffic plus livestock, motor vehicles, machines on wheels, carriages, horse boxes and furniture vans. Goods facilities were not withdrawn until 3rd June, 1968.

Below: K1 2-6-0 No. 62047 from York shed passes Burton Salmon goods yard and heads an Up class K goods towards the Knottingley branch in 1962. *Both Peter Cookson / Neville Stead collection*

Right: The line from Castleford Old Station Junction to Garforth began with a substantial girder bridge which featured two impressive bow lattice spans over the Aire & Calder Navigation. It was still in situ and carrying track in 2001, four years after the line's complete closure.
S. Chapman

CASTLEFORD-GARFORTH & MICKLEFIELD

Below: Two separate pictures have been combined to give a full view of steam locomotives on show outside the NCB's Allerton Bywater workshops on 16th March, 1973. They are from left: *Mexborough*(Hunslet 0-6-0ST 1902 of 1938) *Astley*(Hunslet 0-6-0ST 3509 of 1947), Wheldale Colliery Austerity 0-6-0ST *Antwerp(Hunslet 3180/1944)* **ex-works from overhaul, and an unidentified hulk.** *Steve Chapman*

Transient Block signalling was used between Castleford Old Station Junction and Ledston so that NCB trains could travel over part of the line in mid-section. It is described by former station master David Holmes: "Where the Garforth branch crossed the River Aire, an unusual arrangement applied so that NCB engines could reach the Ledston spoil heaps by crossing the BR bridge. A ground frame on each side and a fairly unique type of block working enabled entrance and exit. This was a Transient Block in which a weak current was passed along one rail and back down the other proving the line to be clear and the ground frames in the normal position. A normal sized lever in the box - a direction lever - was then reversed. Once pulled, only a train from the appropriate end could receive a signal to proceed until the lever was back in the frame when the process could start again."

Above: Inside the National Coal Board's Allerton Bywater workshops on 8th April, 1970 showing the frames of two steam locomotives undergoing overhaul, including Hunslet 2879 which had come from the closed Waterloo Colliery, Leeds. Named *Diana*, No.2879 went on to Wheldale. *Robert Anderson*

Below: Ledston, the first station out of Castleford on the Garforth line looking back towards Castleford on 5th May, 1957. Beyond the overbridge, the NCB spoil tips are to the right while Allerton Bywater workshops had yet to occupy the greenfield site on the left. *P. B. Booth/N. E. Stead collection*

Above: Ledston looking towards Castleford on 5th May, 1957 with the goods yard on the left, the A656 road from Castleford to the A1 at Aberford(the old Castleford-York Roman road Deer Street) going over the bridge, and the Allerton Bywater Colliery sidings on the right. Until 1986 the BR line was also used by NCB trains carrying spoil from Wheldale and Allerton Bywater collieries to tipping grounds beyond the bridge. *P. B. Booth / N. E. Stead collection*

Below: This view from the A656 on 16th May, 1980 shows the busy Allerton Bywater Colliery yard with, left, one of the traditional Hudswell Clarke diesels that were such a feature of this area, and on the right, a Hunslet diesel. The weed-covered BR line from Castleford is on the far right. *Steve Chapman*
Allerton Bywater Colliery closed in March, 1992, ending coal traffic on the line but then trains of merry-go-round hopper wagons with a brake van at each end brought spoil from the Selby mine for dumping on the tipping grounds between Ledston and the River Aire bridge. This lasted until 1996 after which the line was finally taken out of use.

Right: Stored at Allerton Bywater on 24th February, 1979 was Hunslet Austerity 0-6-0ST No. 3168 of 1944. It was rumoured at the time that 3168 was destined for the National Railway Museum in York but it was to see action again at Wheldale first. *Steve Chapman*

Centre: Allerton Bywater Colliery loco shed on 11th June, 1983. The front loco is Barclay No. 42(592/1974) and the next is 46(Hunslet 7408/75) previously at Fryston. The use of standard gauge locos ceased here in 1986. *Adrian Booth*

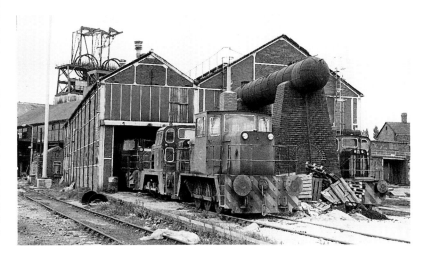

Below: Allerton Main signal box and junction looking towards Garforth on 5th May, 1957 with the line to Primrose Hill Colliery and Bowers Row going off to the left.
P. B. Booth / N. E. Stead collection
The signal box and platform are built of timber to reduce weight on the embankment.
The gradient here meant local instructions governed movements to and from the sidings - the engine must always be on the lower (Ledston) end of the train, no portion of the train must be left on the main line and wagon brakes had to be pinned down for some movements.

The 1969 Appendix showed the 6.25-mile single line from Old Station Jn. to Garforth as signalled by electric token between Ledston and Garforth with the Transient Block between Old Station and Ledston. Signal boxes were at Ledston(1 mile 1214yds from Old Station) and Allerton Main(1 mile 133yds from Ledston.) Down refuge sidings available for trains in either direction were at Ledston and Allerton Main. After closure as a through route the 2 mile 1644yds Ledston -Bowers section was reduced to One Train Working.

Above: Allerton Main signal box and Bowers Halt looking towards Castleford on 5th May, 1957. Built in 1934 to serve new housing, the halt is well kept and still complete with platform seats even though it lost its regular passenger service in 1951. The platform's concrete supports were still in place in 1997. *P. B. Booth / N.Stead collection*

Below: Primrose Hill Colliery on 1st April, 1970 with Hunslet 0-6-0ST *Astley*(3509/47) on its way back from the canal basin to shunt the top yard while an Austerity 0-6-0ST languishes in the background. Primrose Hill closed on 6th March, 1970 but was still washing coal when these pictures were taken. Hunslet 3168 was on the Primrose Hill books around this time. *Robert Anderson*

Above: *Astley* continues its shunting work at Primrose Hill on 1st April, 1970. Three years later *Astley* was lying out of use at Allerton Bywater workshops, as shown on page 42. *Robert Anderson*

Below: *Astley* again, only this time helping out at the Bowers opencast site at 3.52pm on 22nd September, 1969. The opencast was normally worked by an orange and black Austerity belonging to contractors William Pepper & Sons and in the 1970s ex-BR Class 14 No. 9513 was used there by the then contractors Hargreaves. By around 1987 most of the output was leaving by boat and rail traffic ended in 1989. All track beyond Ledston to Bowers was lifted by 1996. *David Holmes*

Above: Next station along the line was Kippax, seen here on 5th May, 1957 looking towards Garforth which was just over three and a quarter miles ahead. The overbridge shows how the line was built for double track but remained mostly single. *P.B.Booth/N.E.Stead collection*

The 1956 Handbook of Stations shows Kippax as equipped to handle parcels, goods traffic, furniture vans, carriages, motor cars, portable engines, machines on wheels, livestock, horse boxes, prize cattle vans, and carriages and motor cars by passenger or parcels train, but it had no permanent crane. Goods facilities were withdrawn with effect from 30th September, 1963. Besides connections via Allerton Main Jn. to Primrose Hill Colliery, private sidings also served Bower(Illingworth) Carbonization Co. and a Ministry of Agriculture, Fisheries and Food store. Even after closure to passengers the station was noted for its prize-winning gardens. In 1968, the Duke of Edinburgh spent the night there on board the Royal Train.

Below: Viewed from the overbridge, Q6 0-8-0 No. 63417 from Leeds Neville Hill shed trundles mineral wagons towards Castleford at 2.3pm on 1st September, 1964. Vandalism and dereliction had yet to take hold on society and the station is well tended despite 13 years of disuse. The goods yard is beyond the platform end, while the signal box on the platform, still bearing its nameboard, is used as a greenhouse. *D. Holmes.*

Above: J6 0-6-0s Nos. 64222 and 64268 from Ardsley shed pass through Kippax station towards Garforth with a Railway Correspondence & Travel Society railtour on 21st September, 1958. The maximum speed on this line was 35mph. *D.Butterfield/N. E. Stead collection*

Below: Although most of the Castleford-Garforth trackbed, indeed some of the track, remained intact in 2001, the site of Garforth Junction where the Castleford line met the Leeds-York line, has changed beyond all recognition since 1960 when Black Fives Nos. 45233 and 45154 *Lanarkshire Yeomanry* were caught at the head of the Newcastle to Manchester Red Bank empty news vans. The junction, signal box and sema-phores are long gone, the cutting on the right has been filled in and the top occupied by commercial premis-es, while the fields on the left and beyond the junction up to the distant woods are occupied by massive housing estates served by their own station, East Garforth, situated near the back of the train. *Peter Cookson*

Above: At 12.25pm on Sunday 25th January, 1959, A3 Pacific No. 60053 *Sansovino* thunders towards Garforth station with the 9.45am Newcastle to Liverpool express. *David Holmes*

The goods yard on the right was equipped to deal with a full range of freight and included a 5-ton yard crane. It closed in the early 1980s, latterly having been used as a car terminal and coal depot. Since then, all track has been stripped to only the two main running lines.

Below: Garforth station in May, 1978 with a Class 40 passing through at the head of a long Leeds-bound coal train. The station buildings on the right have changed little since then except that the canopy has been glazed in to provide an enclosed waiting area. *Robert Anderson*

Above: A mile and three quarters east of Garforth, at the spot where the Roman road Deer Street(the A.656) crosses over the Leeds-York line, there was a station called Ridge Bridge on roughly the same site as an earlier one called Roman Road. Although the station closed in 1914, a year after opening, it remained a fascinating railway location into the 1980s because of the 2ft 6in gauge railway which ran past its buildings, long since converted into a dwelling. The narrow gauge line was operated by the Coal Board and connected Ledston Luck Colliery, a couple of miles along the A656 towards Castleford, with the washery and main line outlet at Peckfield Colliery, Micklefield. On 9th January, 1982 one of the line's Simplex diesel locos passes the former Ridge Bridge station as it leaves Peckfield for Ledston Luck. *Steve Chapman*

Below: On a sunnier 6th January, 1982, a Simplex diesel heads a train of empty tubs alongside the A656 during the run from Peckfield to Ledston Luck. A gradient board shows the line is rising. *Steve Chapman*

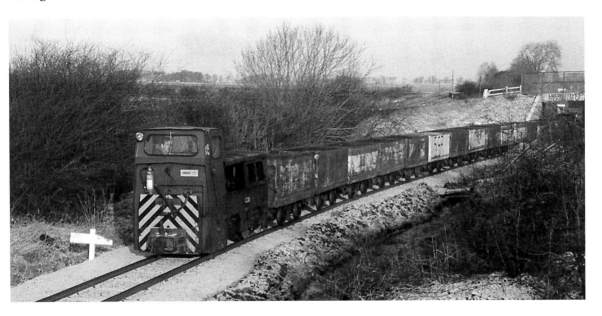

Above: Peckfield Colliery on 28th March, 1972 and what a scene to savour. Peckfield's two working steam locos at that time were, on the left, recently overhauled and immaculate Hunslet 0-6-0ST *Primrose No.2* (3715/52) and, right, the chunky Hudswell Clarke 0-6-0T No. S100 (works No.1822 of 1949.)

Across the Leeds-York main line on the right is Peckfield signal box which outlived the colliery by around 15 years, being closed and demolished in 1999 when control was transferred to Church Fenton(itself since closed and demolished.) *Peter Rose*

Left: Peckfield signal box , its somewhat unusual splitting signal and the colliery sidings looking east on 25th January, 1964. The signal has a NER slotted post on the right but the left hand post has been replaced by the standard upper quadrant type.

The distant on the left is for the York line and the signals on the right are for the Selby line. With the signals for all lines in the "off" position, the box must have been switched out at the time. Also, the nameboard appears to be just about falling off! *David Holmes*

PECKFIELD COLLIERY SIDINGS: When an Up train has work to do in the sidings, no portion of the train must be left on the main line, but the whole of it must be taken inside clear of the main line before shunting operations are commenced. *Eastern Region(Northern Area) Sectional Appendix, 1969.*

Above: S100 looking well cared for at Peckfield on Good Friday 27th March, 1970 while in company with the pit's less fortunate looking 0-6-0 diesel from the same builder, Hudswell Clarke of Leeds.
Both pictures on this page by Robert Anderson

Below: A memorable feature of operations at Peckfield was the thrash up the bank to the quarry where spoil from the colliery was tipped. On 9th July, 1970 Hunslet Austerity 0-6-0ST No. 3891, rebuilt in 1965 with the Hunslet gas producer system, pushes seven loaded Jubilee wagons up the bank from the colliery yard.

The 1956 Stations Handbook shows Micklefield goods yard as having a 3-ton crane and the ability to handle general goods, livestock, horse boxes and prize cattle vans. Goods facilities were withdrawn in February, 1964 but the trackless cattle dock and small goods shed still stood in 2002. Besides Peckfield Colliery, a private siding also served H. Briggs & Son Ltd.

Below: Preserved LMS Black Five 4-6-0 No. 5305 passes through Micklefield station on 30th April, 1977 while en-route from its home at Hull to Leeds where it was picked up an excursion to Carnforth. Since then, the footbridge and boarded crossing have been removed along with platform buildings like those on the left. *Steve Chapman*

SHORT MEMORIES

7.4.62: Deltics and East Coast Pacifics use the Kippax branch when Leeds-Kings Cross services are diverted via Castleford.

September, 1963: New Clayton Type 1 diesel No. D8501 runs loaded mineral trials between Garforth, Castleford, Pontefract and Knottingley.

Above: This wonderful picture by the late Ernie Sanderson shows a seriously workworn D11 4-4-0 heading for the S & K as it strides away from Burton Salmon Junction with a York to Sheffield Victoria express in later LNER or early BR days. Private owner mineral wagons occupy the line from Castleford, one of them lettered Stoke-on-Trent.

BAGHILL & THE S & K

The 1969 BR Sectional Appendix showed the Moorthorpe-Burton Salmon section as signalled by Track Circuit Block with signal boxes at Moorthorpe South, Moorthorpe Station(740yds from South), Pontefract South(6 miles 1441yds from Moorthorpe Stn.), Ferrybridge(2 miles 742yds from Pontefract South) and Burton Salmon(2 miles 188yds from Ferrybridge.) Absolute Block was used south of Moorthorpe. Maximum line speed was 60mph but many temporary speed restrictions were in force due to mining subsidence.

Up and Down goods loops were provided between Moorthorpe South and Station, and at Pontefract Baghill an Up refuge siding to hold 46 wagons, engine and brake van and Down refuge siding to hold 97 wagons, engine and brake van.

FERRYBRIDGE 'A' POWER STATION: Before a propelling movement into Ferrybridge 'A' power station sidings of loaded or empty wagons commences, it must be ensured that one quarter(one fifth of empty wagons) of the wagon brakes are pinned down at the leading end of the train and on completion of the movement a further third(one quarter of empty wagons) of the wagon's brakes next to the locomotive must be applied before the locomotive is detached.

FERRYBRIDGE 'C' POWER STATION: The internal layout consists of an incoming line, leading to two hopper tracks(East and West) which converge at the exit end of the unloading area to form an outgoing line.

A hand worked trailing connection in the incoming line gives access to the Contractor's siding which is on the left of that line. The limit of movement for BR locomotives is defined on the siding by the notice board.

A connection from the East unloading track (exit end) to 'B' power station sidings and 'C' station cripple siding is worked from a ground frame released by Ferrybridge signal box.

BR Eastern Region Sectional Appendix 1969

30.6-1.7.64: 216-ton boiler delivered by rail from Babcock & Wilcox, Glasgow, to Eggborough power station.

February, 1965: Type 4 English Electric diesels begin crew training and clearance tests between Healey Mills and Castleford.

Above: The big 1960s Ferrybridge B and C power stations fed by merry-go-round block coal trains were preceeded by the older, traditional power station, sandwiched between the Knottingley branch and the Aire & Calder Navigation. Besides rail, coal was delivered by barge via a hoist which lifted the laden barges out of the river and into a tippler.

Andrew Barclay 0-4-0ST *Ferrybridge No. 3*(works No.2360 of 1954), was still part of the Central Electricity Generating Board loco fleet at Ferrybridge, though out of use since 1972, when photographed inside the engine shed there on 16th October, 1975. As the shed was right next to the navigation, lifebelts were provided. Robert Stephenson & Hawthorn 0-4-0ST No.23(7795 of 1954) was once at Ferrybridge B. *Adrian Booth* Twenty years later the old power station became the loco and wagon depot for National Power, which took over many power stations upon privatisation of the CEGB and in 1994 began operating its own main line coal trains powered by new Class 59 locomotives in a highly attractive blue and grey livery. National Power later sold its fleet to English Welsh & Scottish Railway and Ferrybridge became an EWS shunter depot.

Below: Against the backdrop of Ferrybridge power station in the 1950s, J39 0-6-0 No.64725 starts onto the S&K proper as it trundles a train of empties through Ferrybridge for Knottingley station on its way from Gascoigne Wood to Frickley Colliery. The Knottingley branch goes off to the right while Ferrybridge goods yard sidings are on the left. Ferrybridge passenger station closed in September, 1965. *Peter Cookson*

Above: The year 1956, and unrebuilt B16 4-6-0 No. 61460 powers past Ferrybridge goods yard and signal box with a southbound Through Freight. Ferrybridge Junction, where the S & K leaves the Burton Salmon-Knottingley branch, is just behind the box. Since 1965 the curve up to the L&Y at Pontefract has diverged to the left. *Both pictures on this page by Peter Cookson*

Back in 1956 Ferrybridge for Knottingley was shown as having a 5-ton crane and the ability to handle general goods, livestock, horse boxes and prize cattle vans, and carriages and motor cars by passenger or parcels train. Goods facilities were withdrawn on 27th April, 1964.

Below: Having just passed through Pontefract Baghill, Beyer-Garratt 2-6-6-2 No. 47993 hauls a northbound load of iron ore on its way from the East Midlands to the blast furnaces of the North East in 1956.

Above: An eagerly awaited train in Pontefract on late 1950s summer evenings was the 2.15pm Tuesday and Friday only class C from Newcastle which carried empty Guinness tankers back to the Park Royal brewery in London. They were road tankers on flat wagons and are seen approaching Baghill hauled by B16/3 No. 61439 at 8.15pm on 31st May, 1957.

Left: Royal Scot No. 46160 *Queen Victoria's Rifleman* descends the curve from Pontefract Monkhill to Baghill with a Leeds Central to London St. Pancras Rugby League cup final special on 13th May, 1961.

Below: Hunslet 0-6-0 shunter D2603 from Ardsley shed comes off the curve from Monkhill with a 1960s trip for Baghill. The curve's viaduct is visible beyond the loco. *All Peter Cookson*

Above: Climbing away from the S & K on the curve to Pontefract Monkhill in 1960, 21A Saltley-based Black Five 4-6-0 No. 44962 heads a Pontefract Races special, probably from the Sheffield area, towards the L & Y line and its destination at Tanshelf station. This train was routed through all three Pontefract stations. *Peter Cookson*

Below: With the line to Monkhill on its right, Class 04/5 2-8-0 No. 63745 heads north from Pontefract Baghill with a Class H Through Freight from the Great Central section in about 1956.
Only a handful of Great Central 2-8-0s were rebuilt in the 1930s as 04/5 by fitting a shortened Gresley 02 boiler with separate smokebox saddle. Of the four survivors in 1955, two(including 63745) had been scrapped and two rebuilt as Class 04/8 by the start of the 1960s. *Peter Cookson*

Above: York A2/3 Pacific No. 60512 *Steady Aim* passes the derelict Pontefract signal box while leaving Baghill station with a Pontefract to Newcastle bank holiday relief on 18th May, 1959. This train ran instead of the usual Birmingham to Newcastle which did not run on bank holidays and around 200 people caught it at Baghill. The loco brought the empty stock tender first from York because it was too big for the Baghill turntable. The points in front of 60512 mark the start of the line up to Monkhill. Comparison with the lay-out diagram on page 67 reveals that the pointwork, consisting of a trailing crossover and single lead, had been simplified in 1956 from a double line crossover with two slips. *Peter Cookson*

Below: Another Selby engine, Q1 0-8-0T No. 69933, and a Q6 pass the Baghill station Up side buildings at some time around 1958. It is thought the Great Central Railway-design Q1, used for hump shunting at Gascoigne Wood yard, was probably on its way to Gorton Works in Manchester. *Peter Tait*

Baghill station from the south end as the 3.50pm Newcastle to Birmingham express calls there in 1958. The leading engine is Jubilee 4-6-0 No. 45725 *Repulse* with a Black Five 4-6-0 behind it. Rising up to the right is Bag Hill from which the station took its name when renamed from just Pontefract in 1936. *Peter Cookson*

PONTEFRACT BAGHILL PASSENGER TRAIN DEPARTURES SUMMER, 1955

Down direction

am

8.0		7.5 Sheffield Midland-York local
8.11	SO	7.12 Sheffield Victoria-Bridlington *Until 20th August*
8.46	SO	7.56 Sheffield Midland-Scarborough
9.8		8.17 Sheffield Victoria-Scarborough
10.31	SO	9.40 Sheffield Victoria-York
10.47		8.5 Birmingham-Newcastle

pm

12.2	SO	7.55 Manchester London Road-Scarborough. *Until 3rd Sept.*
12.18		7.54 Worcester-York
3.53		3pm Sheffield Midland-York local
4.24		12.58 Banbury/8.15 Swansea MSO - York/Newcastle FO.
4.52		7.45 Paignton-Newcastle
6.47		5.50 Sheffield Midland-York local
7.0		11.16 Bournemouth West-Newcastle
7.30	SX	11.5 Paignton-York
7.39	SO	2.15 Bristol-York
10.4	SO	11.0 Newquay-York
10.27	SX	4.45 Bristol-York
11.5		Empty stock to Selby

Up direction

am

8.6		7.20 York-Sheffield Midland local
9.51	SO	7.30 Newcastle-Paignton
10.12		9.42 York/7.42 SunderlandSO-Sheffield Mid. *To Birmingham SO and M-F in high summer.*
10.35		8.15 Newcastle-Bristol/Cardiff SO.
10.54		8.37 Newcastle-Bournemouth West

pm

12.31		11.48 York-Sheffield Midland local
12.40	SO	10.0 Scarborough-Manchester London Road
12.50		12.20 York-Banbury/Swansea MFO
1.4		12.30 York-Bristol
1.45	SO	1pm York-Sheffield Midland local
2.54		12.37 Newcastle-Bristol
3.10	SO	1.17 Bridlington-Sheffield Victoria. *Until 10/9*
4.0	SO	2.23 Scarborough-Sheffield Midland. *Until 10/9*
5.7		4.15 York-Sheffield Midland local
6.10		3.57 Newcastle-Birmingham/Penzance FO
7.56		7.15 York-Sheffield Midland local
9.39	FO	6.52 Newcastle-Birmingham
10.9		7.5 Newcastle-Bristol
10.58		10.22 York-Swindon/Bristol SO

In summer 2002 just the following called at Pontefract Baghill: 09.27, 13.35 and 21.31SX Sheffield-York locals, and the 11.13 and 15.05 York-Sheffield locals(slightly different times on Saturdays.)

Pontefract Baghill-battery tail lamps. The guard of an incoming train must remove tail lamp before train enters depot and take it to signalman for safe keeping. The guard of an outgoing train is responsible for collecting lamp from signalman and for placing it on train after it has drawn out of depot...*Sectional Appendix supplement, October, 1975*

Above: Baghill station's Down side buildings and split-level platform looking south in August, 1988. The station became unstaffed on 28th November that year when the ticket office was closed, the buildings since being converted into private offices. *Malcolm Roughley*

Below: The 12.48pm York to Bristol was typical of the North East-South West expresses which plied the Swinton & Knottingley in steam days and staple motive power included Patriot and Jubilee 4-6-0s from 82E Bristol Barrow Road shed. Here, Patriot No. 45506 *The Royal Pioneer Corps* starts the train away from Pontefract Baghill in October 1960. *Peter Cookson*

SHORT MEMORIES

14.5.65: Jubilee 45565 *Victoria* heads a Saturday Castleford-Bridlington excursion.

2.66: The York-Poole train is steam again, foreign Black Fives 44871, 44942 and 45331 among the locos powering it.

3.4.66: Colour light signalling commissioned between Pontefract Baghill and Moorthorpe to accommodate increasing merry-go-round coal trains. It is controlled automatically by track circuits and from Pontefract South and Moorthorpe boxes. Brackenhill box is closed. Colour light signals already in use between Ferrybridge and Pontefract.

The next three pictures illustrate the variety of 4-4-0s which could be seen on S & K passenger services up to the end of the 1950s.

Above: Midland 2P 4-4-0 No. 40538 brings the 9.40am Saturdays Only Sheffield Midland to York local into Baghill as Q6 0-8-0 No. 63451 waits in the yard with the returning Brackenhill goods. Pontefract South signal box is on the left. *Peter Cookson*

Below: Ex-Great Central D11/1 "Large Director" 4-4-0 No. 62663 *Prince Albert* leaves Baghill for Sheffield Victoria with the 12.20pm York to Banbury express. *Peter Cookson*

Above: Class D49/2 No. 62751 *The Albrighton*, the most common of all Scarborough-based D49s at Baghill, sets off with the Sunday 12.15pm York to Bristol. The smokebox door reads train No. 322 but this is not train 322. *Peter Cookson*

Below: Viewed from Pontefract South signal box towards the end of the 1950s, B16/3 4-6-0 No. 61439 passes Baghill goods yard and digs into the 1 in 152 climb away from the station while heading a southbound Through Freight. *Peter Cookson*

Above: Royal Scot 4-6-0 No. 46131 *The Royal Warwickshire Regiment* from 41C Sheffield Millhouses shed provides ample power for the four-coach 1pm Saturdays Only York to Sheffield Midland stopper, seen passing NER slotted signals as it departs Baghill. The picture is undated but this engine was reported to have worked this train on 30th July, 1960. *Peter Cookson*

Below: With Pontefract South box on the right and the goods sheds on the left, 8F 2-8-0 No. 48205 coasts down into Baghill station at tenpast eight on a fine late-1950s morning with a northbound load of iron ore as Jubilee 4-6-0 No. 45660 *Rooke* heaves its heavy 7.20am York-Sheffield stopper onto the southbound gradient. How the S & K has declined. In 2002, such trains as *Rooke* is hauling consist of nothing more than a basic railcar, probably just a single vehicle Class 153; the goods yard and signal box are gone and the sun seems to shine nowhere near as much! However, the line does still see a few heavy freights each day. *Peter Cookson*

Above: Elegant ex-Midland Railway 0-6-0s meet in Baghill goods yard sometime around 1957 while working local trip freights from Canklow, near Rotherham. On the turntable road on the left, working trip 120, is Deeley 3F No. 43814 while on the right with trip 123 is Johnson 2F No. 58198 of a class originally dating from 1875, though 58198 was rebuilt some time after 1917 with a Belpaire firebox. *Peter Cookson*

Below: Heavy work for a member of the footplate crew of Q6 No. 63406 on Brackenhill duty as he pushes it round on Baghill goods yard's manual turntable. Trains from the Brackenhill branch went to Baghill yard for initial sorting before continuing to Gascoigne Wood. They were nearly always worked by a Selby Q6 until that shed's closure in 1959 after which they were worked by York engines. *Peter Cookson*

Right: The purpose of this one-ton container marked "Return to Pontefract" seen inside a transparent-sided 12-ton van at York is a mystery. The van appears to be otherwise full of rubbish.
Ernest Sanderson / Steve Chapman collection

Pontefract Baghill was equipped to handle the full range of goods traffic including furniture vans, carriages, motor cars, portable engines, machines on wheels, livestock, horse boxes, prize cattle vans and carriages and motor cars by passenger or parcels train. The goods yard crane was of 5-ton capacity.

Goods facilities were withdrawn on 2nd November, 1964 and in 2002 the goods yard site was occupied by a firm dealing in containers and portable cabins.

Below: Pontefract Baghill layout in 1893.
Not to scale

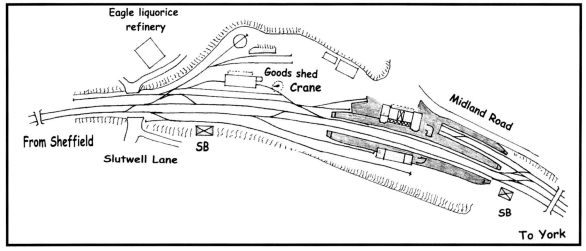

Right: Another rebuilt Johnson Midland 2F 0-6-0 from Canklow at Baghill goods yard, No. 58238. A loco coal wagon stands in the background.
G. W. Sharpe collection

In 1950 the return fare to London from Pontefract was 46s 9d third class(£2.34) and 70s 2d first class(£3.51.)

Above: Another sample of the rich variety of traffic once using the S&K. A class C banana special hauled by rebuilt B16 4-6-0 No. 61420 coasts down grade and over bridge No. 25 towards Baghill sometime in the late 1950s. The vans are marked "Steam Bananas" which doubtless means they are steam heated in the same way as passenger stock. *Peter Cookson*

Below: More 4-4-0 variety at Pontefract Baghill. This time it's one of the Compounds of Midland Railway design. Despite looking rather workstained, LMS-built No. 41048 combines power and elegance as it charges the bank away from the station in August, 1958 with a races special believed to be from York. *Peter Cookson*

Above: No. 41190 similarly storms the bank away from Baghill with the 1pm Saturday Only York-Sheffield Midland local on 12th January, 1957. *Peter Cookson*

Below: Trip No. 123 from Canklow with 2F 0-6-0 No. 58170 in charge nears journey's end at Pontefract Baghill in 1956. *Peter Cookson / Neville Stead collection*

Above: D49/2 4-4-0 No. 62762 *The Fernie* from 50D Starbeck shed makes a splendid sight on a crisp day in December, 1958 as it blasts away from Baghill with the Sunday 12.15pm York-Bristol. *Peter Cookson*

Below: Shades of the old Somerset & Dorset only this is Yorkshire. A truly classic scene south of Pontefract and another illustration of motive power variety which graced the S&K in the 1950s. Here, 2P 4-4-0 No. 40513 from 17A Derby shed pilots Black Five 4-6-0 No. 45428 at the head of the heavily loaded 12.43pm Newcastle-Bristol, the 2.56pm from Baghill. *Peter Cookson*

Above: More classic power south of Pontefract in 1957. D11/1 4-4-0 No. 62666 *Zeebrugge* smokes its way up the 1 in 152 with 11 coaches on the Fridays and Saturdays Only 12.20pm York-Swansea, a train which ran only as far as Banbury the rest of the week. *Peter Cookson*

Below: Q6 0-8-0 No. 63432 leaves Pontefract in about 1958 and makes for the Brackenhill Light Railway with a trip working from Baghill. *Peter Cookson*

Above: On a summer's day in the late 1950s, the now preserved Q6 No. 63395 heads towards Pontefract from the south with what is thought to be the 6.20am Dewsnap to Gascoigne Wood class H Through Freight.

Below: A couple of miles south of Pontefract was Ackworth station, seen here looking north c1960. Although the passenger station closed in July, 1951 and goods facilities were withdrawn on 1st August, 1955, 20 months after being downgraded to a public delivery siding, the station remained intact, right down to the platform seats. The disused signal box is at the far end of the Up platform on the right and the abandoned goods shed, track all removed, on the left. The trackless and isolated goods shed still stood in 2002. *Both Peter Cookson*

Above: Protected by well-kept NER slotted signals, this was Brackenhill Junction where the light railway left the S&K, viewed from a southbound express on 29th August, 1962. The Brackenhill branch closed that January but in 2002 the embankment curving away from the main line was still clearly visible. *Peter Rose*

Below: Looking towards the terminus of the Brackenhill Light Railway at Hemsworth Colliery. The line of wagons on the horizon marks the Doncaster-Leeds line. *Peter Cookson*

Above: An old tar boiler grabs the attention along with a solitary slotted distant signal at Ackworth Moor Top. The cranes on the horizon though are evidence of the quarries which produced high quality grindstones which in earlier years were despatched by rail from this goods station. *Peter Cookson*

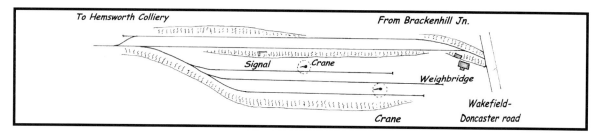

Above: The layout at Ackworth Moor Top as it was in 1919. *Not to scale*

The 1956 Handbook of Stations listed Ackworth Moor Top as equipped with 10-ton cranage but with facilities to handle only general goods traffic.

Right: A Brackenhill Light Railway milepost at Ackworth Moor Top. *Peter Cookson*

74

SHORT MEMORIES

13.2.67: The new order kicks in with a big increase in merry-go-round coal trains to Ferrybridge C power station hauled by specially adapted Class 47 diesels.

25.3.67: Low-speed Class 47s D1894/5/1994/5/6/7 allocated to new depot at Knottingley. Shunters D2313/9 follow by 22/4

Above: A long-winded S&K trespass warning at Moorthorpe Junction on 29th August, 1962 where the connecting spur from the Doncaster-Leeds line at South Kirkby joins the S&K. Beyond the signals is the alignment of the abandoned north-facing spur from South Elmsall to the S&K which could be reopened in the early 21st century as part of a new East Coast trunk freight route, of which the northern half of the S&K would become part. *Peter Rose*

Below: Moorthorpe station looking south in the late 1950s, superbly-kept as was much of the railway system in those pre-Beeching years. Station master Douglas Clegg stands, justifiably proud, on his lawn behind the Down platform while the signalman tries hard to get into the picture from the window of his Moorthorpe Station cabin on the Up platform. *Peter Cookson/N. E. Stead collection*
The station presented a very different scene in 2002. Although still served by Leeds and York-Sheffield trains, the main buildings were derelict after many years' use as the Mallard pub, while the Up side buildings and signal box were long gone. A signal box survived at Moorthorpe South along with the loops visible just beyond the overbridge, but the much-cherished lawn had become a car park.

THE LANKY LINES

Above: The Lancashire & Yorkshire Methley-Pontefract line looking across the three-arch River Calder viaduct towards Lofthouse Junction and signal box at Methley on the 24th July, 1980. The Methley Joint line, by then going only as far as Newmarket Colliery, can be seen curving away left opposite the box while the line to Methley Junction and Leeds continues straight ahead.

The trackless viaduct survives in 2002.

Peter Rose

The LMS 1937 Sectional Appendix shows the Pontefract-Methley line as signalled by Absolute Block. Signal boxes(with distance from previous box) were at Prince of Wales Siding(409yds from Pontefract), Glasshoughton East (1mile 575yds), Glasshoughton West (614yds), Cutsyke Jn.(937yds), Castleford Station(444yds - not a block post), Whitwood Sidings(1171yds), Lofthouse Jn.(1050yds), Methley Stn.(788yds) and Methley Jn. (248yds.) A Down Goods line ran from Prince of Wales Sdg. to Pontefract.

Above: The Methley-Pontefract line at Whitwood with English Electric Type 4 No. 40007 about to cross the bridge over the NER York-Altofts line while heading towards Pontefract on 24th July, 1980. This line was closed and lifted just three years later but in recent times there has been talk of reinstating it to provide a dedicated freight route between Doncaster and the busy Freightliner terminal at Stourton, Leeds. *Peter Rose*

ALL TRAINS working traffic off the Methley Joint line between Lofthouse and Methley must stop at Castleford (LMS) for number taking. *LMS Central Division Sectional Appendix, 1937.*

WHITWOOD SIDINGS: Wagons not coupled to a locomotive must not be left on the Up main line between the Up Home and Starting signals. Wagons from the colliery sidings must be placed on the Down main line and the locomotive must run round via the Up main. *BR NE Region Sectional Appendix, 1960.*

Above: An extensive industrial network serving Whitwood Colliery and various coal products plants was once connected to the L&Y just east of the intersection bridge. Among the fascinating array of locomotives once working this system were these ex-NER Class 964 0-6-0STs, six of which were sold to Briggs Collieries of Whitwood between 1906 and 1909,the last of them believed to have been scrapped at Water Haigh Colliery, Leeds, in 1955.

In the absence of a picture of a Whitwood example, *Mars,* a member of the same class at Seaham Harbour, County Durham, is shown here. *Neville Stead collection*

Whitwood Colliery closed in 1968 and by the early 1970s the only railway left was the 2ft gauge system of Cawoods' briquetting plant and its Hunslet-built diesel.

Below: Castleford's station on the L&Y was the rather modest affair at Cutsyke which was served by Goole-Knottingley-Leeds trains. Cutsyke station closed on 7th October, 1968 when these services were rerouted via a reversal at Central station. Here, Ivatt Class 2 2-6-0 No. 46493 from 55A Leeds Holbeck shed arrives at Cutsyke with the 1.10pm Knottingley-Leeds on 9th July, 1960. Cutsyke Junction signal box is just visible in the distance along with the spoil heaps of Glasshoughton Colliery. *D. P. Leckonby*

Above: Travelling towards Pontefract the next big industrial complex was at Glasshoughton where this was the view of Glasshoughton Colliery engine shed as roughly seen from a Castleford-Pontefract train. With the headgear standing proud, Hudswell Clarke 0-6-0T No. S118(1870/1953) and Hunslet 0-6-0ST GH No.4(3855/54) stand outside the shed at 1.35pm on 20th April, 1972. The locomotives became redundant when a new rapid loading bunker was commissioned in the early 1970s, though Austerity saddletank Hunslet 2868 of 1943 from the neighbouring coke works was stored there until March, 1979. The colliery closed in 1986.*David Holmes*

GLASSHOUGHTON SIGNAL BOX. Colliery Sidings: When trains have to call at Glasshoughton Colliery and vehicles have to be left on either the Up or Down main lines, the vehicles left on the main lines must be securely held by the van brake being put hard on, and in addition the brakes of 1 in 10 wagons must be pinned down. *BR NE Region Sectional Appendix, 1960.*

Below: The steaming and smoking mass of Glasshoughton coke works on 15th August, 1977 by which time its Hawthorn Leslie 0-6-0ST *Coal Products No.3* was out of use and stood on a siding with two coke cars. It is quite alarming how such a big industrial complex can be made to disappear as totally as it has done since closing in March, 1978 due to the low demand for coke caused by recession in the steel industry. In 2002 this vast site was being redeveloped. *Adrian Booth*

Above: The stylish blue-liveried Hawthorn Leslie 0-6-0ST *Coal Products No.3*, pictured here on 24th June, 1975, continued to deputise for the diesels until 1977 when it needed retubing, work which was never undertaken by its then owners, National Smokeless Fuels Ltd. It was moved away for preservation on the Tanfield Railway, County Durham, in March, 1979. *Adrian Booth*

Below: Local collieries were served by trips from Gascoigne Wood powered by Selby engines. Here, Q6 0-8-0 No. 63448 hauls an afternoon working towards Pontefract in the 1950s. The train had run via Castleford and was on its way to Pontefract Monkhill where it would reverse and continue to Sharlston Colliery on the Wakefield line. *Peter Cookson*

Sunk in 1870, Prince of Wales was destined to become the oldest colliery in Yorkshire by 2002 when it closed. These pictures show but three of the locos which once worked there.

Top: Hudswell Clarke 0-6-0T No. S120(1886 of 1955) working the yard on 8th April, 1970. *Robert Anderson*

Standard gauge locomotive work ended in 1977 after completion of a rapid loading bunker and the last standard gauge loco, Hunslet diesel 6685 left in July, 1979 when it was transferred to Wheldale.

By 1982 the Prince of Wales pit had been converted to a drift mine operated by a 2ft 6 in gauge internal railway.

Centre: Out of use on 2nd May, 1959 was *Halkon*, a Manning Wardle 0-6-0ST works No. 1448 of 1899. This engine was originally on the Goole & Marshland Railway(*Railway Memories No.14*) and was named after its chairman. In 1901 it was involved in a fatal collision and later sold to Glasshoughton & Castleford Collieries being sold on to Prince of Wales Colliery. *Halkon* was scrapped in 1961. *Neville Stead*

Left: By 1974 a loco crisis caused by diesel failures saw this Austerity 0-6-0ST built in 1944 by Bagnalls of Stafford, works No. 2746, repaired and put back to work in their place. It is seen drawing up internal wagons in the colliery yard opposite Prince of Wales Colliery signal box on 12th May, 1976. *Steve Chapman*

Above: From the start of merry-go-round coal workings in the 1960s until 1980, Class 47s based at Knottingley were used for such operations. Here, No. 47324 passes Prince of Wales Colliery box heading in the Castleford direction with empties during the 1970s. Despite being almost destroyed by fire in the mid-1990s, this was one of the few remaining traditional boxes left in the area in 2002. *Peter Cookson*

SHORT MEMORIES

March, 1967: WD and 8F 2-8-0s, B1 4-6-0s and 9F 2-10-0s still have command of Wakefield-Goole line freight despite an influx of Class 37 diesels from Healey Mills, York and Hull depots.

22.4.67: Jubilee 45593 *Kolhapur* travels over the Kippax branch with an enthusiasts' special.

2.5.67: BR Class 3 2-6-0 No. 77012 takes a chocolate and cream inspection saloon along the Wakefield-Pontefract line.

Below: Crofton East where the L&Y line from Goole reaches the outskirts of Wakefield and where a spur climbs up to join the former Midland main line from Leeds to Derby. Here, on 28th May, 1994, one of West Yorkshire's Class 141 Leyland railbuses working a Pontefract Monkhill to Wakefield service passes the entrance to the closed Crofton permanent way depot. The railbuses, which suffered a host of mechanical problems, have all since been withdrawn but the site has been converted into a maintenance and testing depot for the new Voyager-type trains.

There was once a station at Crofton but it closed to passengers way back in 1931 and to goods in 1952. *Steve Chapman*

Left: The Up platform of Sharlston station remained intact on Monday 5th March, 2001 when being passed by a Class 66 diesel heading a freight from Monk Bretton, near Cudworth, to Doncaster. Sharlston Colliery was over on the right until its closure in May, 1993.

Sharlston station dated from around 1869 when it was opened to serve the West Riding's first purpose-built mining village at New Sharlston. It closed to both passengers and goods in March, 1958. When the new Wakefield-Pontefract service was introduced in May, 1992 a new halt was opened at Streethouse, 600 yards further east. *Steve Chapman*

SHARLSTON COLLIERY: Up or Down trains from Sharlston Colliery must not draw up to the outlet signal until the line is clear for a straight run onto the main line. Trap points operated by the NCB crossing keeper are provided in each siding and trains must when possible stand in the rear of the trap points and clear of the public highway. When trains in the colliery sidings cannot stand clear of the public highway they must be divided, leaving the highway clear until such time as the line is clear to run onto the main line. *BR Sectional Appendix, 1960.*

A supplement of May, 1970 gave new instructions in connection with the operation of the rapid loading bunker. The bunker was commissioned in April, 1968 but in January, 1969 it collapsed, dropping 1500 tons of coal on to a train which was loading at the time.

Below: Ackton Hall Colliery at Featherstone held a remarkable variety of steam locomotives into the mid-1970s, especially as they were mainly for standby to the dominant diesels. With one of the said diesels lurking in the background, out of use Peckett inside-cylinder 0-6-0ST *Ackton Hall No. 3(1567/1920)* heads a line-up which also includes Austerity 0-6-0STs 143(Bagnall 2740 of 1944) and S112(Hunslet 2414 of 1941) at 12.27pm on 15th September, 1972. No. 2740 was sold for scrap but the other two locos both made it into preservation. *David Holmes*

ACKTON HALL COLLIERY SIDINGS: LNE mineral trains may be allowed to work not more than four loaded wagons from Ackton Hall Colliery to Sharlston, so as to save stopping on the return journey. When the wagons exceed four, they must be worked direct to Pontefract. *LMS Central Division Sectional Appendix, 1937.*

Above: Two and a half years after the BR Eastern Region's last steam goods train had passed through Featherstone on its way to Goole, steam was still very much alive at Ackton Hall Colliery. On 8th April, 1970, No. 143 on the right was joined by Hunslet 0-6-0ST No. S119 *Beatrice*(2705 of 1945) outside the engine shed. *Beatrice* is reported to have last been used here in autumn, 1975. *Robert Anderson*

Ackton Hall still had no less than five steam locos on its books in 1973. They were: Peckett 1567, *Airedale* (Hunslet 1440), Hunslet 2414, No. 143 - all out of use at the time - and *Beatrice* on standby for failed diesels.

Right: The end of steam at Ackton Hall. It's last remaining steam loco, Austerity 0-6-0ST Bagnall 2746 of 1944 stands forlorn amid a pile of scrap high above the disused Down platform of the old Featherstone station on 9th January, 1982. Never used since moving from Prince of Wales in 1977, it was the last steam loco at a Yorkshire colliery when it left for preservation at PeakRail, Matlock, on 4th October, 1983.

The high level line on which it is standing once formed a connection from the main line at a point east of the Castleford-Featherstone road which it crossed over on a bridge parallel with the main line level crossing. Ackton Hall closed in 1985 without resuming production after the 1984/85 miners' strike. *Steve Chapman*

Above: A mile and a half east of Featherstone comes Pontefract where the first station is Tanshelf. Ex- L & Y Apsinall 3F 0-6-0 No. 52305, wearing a Goole 53E shedplate, has just passed the station and signal box with the evening Goole to Wakefield pick-up in the late 1950s. *Peter Cookson*

Below: Pontefract Tanshelf looking east in April,1955 with a once common railway feature, a trackside allotment, on the left and the bay platform and goods yard on the right. Ivatt Class 2 2-6-2T No. 41253 from 25A Wakefield shed departs with the 12.25pm Goole to Wakefield stopping service. *Peter Cookson*

Above: Goole-based Fowler 2-6-4T No. 42407 makes an awesome sight as it blasts out of Tanshelf with the 7.57am Knottingley to Wakefield and Bradford local in 1957. *Peter Cookson*

Below: The Wakefield-Goole line's premier train in the 1950s was the Wakefield-Hull express which ran non-stop between Wakefield and Goole but for a call at Snaith on Saturdays. Here, one of Goole's Stanier Class 4 2-6-4Ts, No. 42553, speeds the 11.48am from Wakefield through Tanshelf on a summer's day in the mid-1950s. Nowadays, only local trains use the line. *Peter Cookson*

Goods facilities at Pontefract Tanshelf were minimal compared with the town's other two stations. The yard was equipped to handle only general goods traffic and had no permanent crane. It closed when the passenger station was made unstaffed on 6th November, 1961.

Above: Tanshelf's bay platform sees use as ex-Midland Railway 4F 0-6-0 No. 43998 from 18B Westhouses shed in the East Midlands awaits home-going punters with a Pontefract races special during summer, 1956. The train will travel via Crofton and the curve to the Midland main line. *Peter Cookson / G. W. Sharpe collection*

Below: Another classic Midland design, LMS-built 2P 4-4-0 No. 40630 from Normanton shed puts in an appearance at Tanshelf in September, 1955 with the 4.30pm Goole to Bradford Exchange, composed of low-roof suburban stock. *Peter Cookson*

Above: A young admirer stands rooted to the spot as Fowler 2-6-4T No. 42406 from 56D Mirfield shed arrives in Tanshelf station with the 6pm Goole to Wakefield during 1957. *Peter Cookson*

Below: Liverpool Bank Hall Jubilee No. 45717 *Dauntless* was more likely to be seen at Castleford on the Liverpool Exchange-Newcastle express during the week but on this summer Saturday in 1960 it rattled the various platform fitments while thundering through Tanshelf with the Saturdays Only Scarborough-Liverpool Exchange. The baggage van behind the engine illustrates consideration that holidaymakers carry large amounts of luggage, a fact which often seems to escape some present day railway managers when it comes to planning new trains. *Peter Cookson*

Above: Ivatt Class 2 2-6-0 No. 46408 makes a smoky entrance to Tanshelf station with the 4.30pm Goole to Bradford Exchange during September, 1955. This whole scene disappeared during 1967, with the station closing in January and the last steam train, the 15.00 Carlton to Goole freight, passing through on 4th November hauled by Royston 8F 2-8-0 No. 48276.
Peter Cookson

Below: The rather uninspiring street approach to the old Tanshelf station, as it was in the 1950s. *Peter Cookson*

SHORT MEMORIES

13.5.67: Featherstone station, closed in January, reopens for five special trains to the Rugby League cup final at Wembley.

18.5.67: Unique Black Five 4-6-0 No. 44767 hauls four withdrawn LMR steam locos along the Wakefield-Goole line while on their way to a Hull scrapyard. 44767 returns to the LMR later in the day.

21.5.67: WD No. 90404 hauls Jubilees 45565, 45694 and 45739, and 9F 2-10-0 92116 over the Wakefield-Goole line en-route to scrap in Hull.

Above: Passing the site of the present day Tanshelf station in early 1957 is Ivatt Class 2 2-6-0 No. 46408 while leaving the previous station with the 9.20am Wakefield to Goole. *Peter Cookson*

Below: Generators and regenerators. With the cooling towers of Ferrybridge power station forming a backdrop early in 1992 the partly-built new Tanshelf station, viewed from the overbridge dividing it from the site of the previous station, is shaken by the Drax to Lindsey empty oil tanks headed by original generator-equipped Class 47 No. 47401, restored to 1960s two-tone green livery as D1500. Passenger services were being reinstated to help regenerate the local economy in the wake of widespread pit closures. *Steve Chapman*

Above: Looking west from the footbridge at Pontefract Monkhill towards Pontefract West Junction and signal box. The main line to Tanshelf and Wakefield goes straight ahead while the line to Methley and Castleford curves to the right with Prince of Wales Colliery just out of view. Nowadays the signal box and semaphores are no more, the cattle dock siding on the left is gone while the goods lines and sidings on the right have been thinned down to just two roads. *Peter Cookson*

Below: Looking from Pontefract West Junction towards Monkhill station on 4th May, 1957. Ivatt 2-6-0 No. 46493 of 55A Leeds Holbeck shed heads the 1pm Saturdays Only Knottingley to Leeds service onto the line that will take it via Cutsyke and Methley. The 8F 2-8-0, No. 48622, has brought a coal train from Whitwood. Midland Division locos like 48622 tended to work coal from the Methley line as far as Pontefract where it was taken forward to Goole or Crofton Hall sidings by Central Division WD 2-8-0s. *Peter Cookson*

Above: Less customary power for a pick-up goods on the L&Y. Ex-Great Central Class O4/7 2-8-0 No. 63857 from 56B Ardsley shed trundles a short westbound trip working through Monkhill station and towards the Wakefield line in 1962. No. 63857 was one of a batch rebuilt by the LNER under Sir Nigel Gresley with a Class O2-type boiler but retaining its original Great Central smokebox. *P. Cookson / G. W. Sharpe collection*

Below: The more usual pick-up of the 1950s. In 1955, one of the Aspinall 3F 0-6-0s rebuilt with a Belpaire firebox and extended smokebox, Goole's No. 52273, heads through Pontefract Monkhill with the Knottingley-Wakefield trip which includes an ex-North British Railway brake van. *Peter Cookson / N. E. Stead collection*

Above: Pontefract Monkhill station looking west in the early 1960s. Since then the buildings have been swept away, the platforms shortened and the footbridge replaced by a modern structure. Just one shelter is now provided, on the Up platform.

On weekdays in summer, 1957 Monkhill was served by 29 trains a day, to Wakefield, Leeds via Cutsyke, Baghill, and Knottingley or Goole. In June, 2002 it was served by 63 trains a day to Wakefield, Leeds via Castleford, and Knottingley but only two to Goole. *Both pictures on this page by Peter Cookson*

Below: An L&Y 0-6-0 simmers in the yard as 2-6-4T No. 42407 hurries the 6.35pm Hull to Wakefield express through Monkhill station. In 1957 this train was allowed just 35 minutes for the 27.25 miles from Goole to Wakefield where it connected with the 8pm to Liverpool. On summer Fridays it ran through to Liverpool.

Above: When considerable amounts of freight still ran on Saturdays. WD 2-8-0 No. 90135 proudly displaying a clean smokebox starts out from Monkhill on 4th May, 1957 with a load of coal for Crofton Hall sidings, near Wakefield. This was the sort of train brought in by the 8F on page 90. A distant L&Y 0-6-0 shunts the goods yard on the right. *Both pictures on this page by Peter Cookson*

Below: Looking east from Monkhill station in the 1950s with a L&Y 0-6-0 shunting the evening pick-up in the busy goods yard as the shunter or guard converses with someone in the goods office. Note the vintage signal behind which half the train is standing on the main line. The goods yard closed in July, 1970 and has been abandoned though the siding nearest the main line remained in 2002 together with a loop on the left.

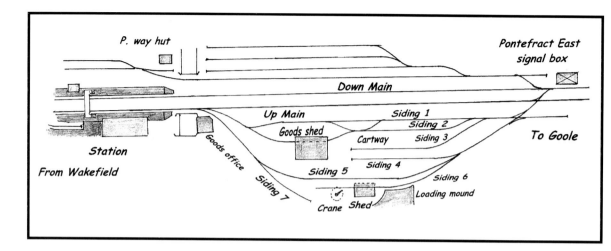

Above: The layout at Pontefract Monkhill goods yard taken from a BR drawing dated 5th July, 1968 when siding No.7 and the points connecting siding No.5 to the Up Main were being abandoned. The yard once included three roads sprouting at right angles from wagon turntables in the siding next to the main line. *Not to scale*

The 1956 Handbook of Stations showed Pontefract Monkhill goods yard as equipped with a 10-ton crane and able to handle the full range of freight, including furniture vans, motor cars, carriages, machines on wheels, livestock, horse boxes and prize cattle vans, and carriages and motor cars by passenger or parcels train.

Below: Substantial power for the Knottingley-Wakefield pick-up on 9th April, 1959 was ex-LMS Fowler 7F 0-8-0 No. 49618 from 26C Bolton shed. It appears that a wagon of pit props is being detached. Trains regularly brought pit props from Hull or Goole to the yard here from whence they were tripped to Prince of Wales Colliery by the local pilot. The old signal in the previous picture has been replaced by a standard BR upper quadrant type. *Peter Cookson/Neville Stead collection*

Above: Pontefract Monkhill goods from the east end in the 1950s with Ivatt 2-6-0 No. 46415 on pick-up duty and two ancient 4-wheel coaches no doubt in use by the engineer's department. *Peter Cookson*

SHORT MEMORIES

June, 1967: 8F 2-8-0s still working Royston-Goole freights through Pontefract Monkhill.

June, 1967: The summer Saturday Castleford-Blackpool, a regular Jubilee in 1966, is now a Class 40 diesel. It will eventually be a DMU.

3.6.67: Steam working on the Wakefield-Goole line declines following closure of Wakefield shed.

23.6.67: Immaculate B1 61306 seen heading west through Featherstone light engine.

December, 1967: Leeds-Kings Cross trains diverted via Wakefield, Knottingley and Askern.

The 1937 LMS Sectional Appendix showed the line between Crofton East and Hensall as signalled by Absolute Block with signal boxes at(with distance from previous box): Sharlston Station(1 mile 1052yds from Crofton East), Streethouse West(602yds), Red Lane Level Crossing(367yds - not a block post), Snydale West(402yds), Snydale East(792yds), Featherstone Colliery(855yds), Featherstone Station(692yds), Pontefract Tanshelf(1 mile 1285yds), Pontefract West(1359yds), Pontefract East(650yds), Knottingley A(1 mile 880yds), Knottingley B(528yds), Knottingley Depot West(711yds), England Lane Level Crossing(164yds-not a block post), Knottingley Depot East(463yds), Sudforth Lane(1 mile 1382yds), Whitley Bridge(1 mile 1084yds), Hensall(1 mile 1344yds), Heck Ings Level Crossing(1 mile 14yds -not a block post), Hensall Jn.(626yds.)

Extra running lines on this stretch were Up and Down Goods Snydale West-Featherstone Stn., Down Goods Pontefract West-East, Up and Down Slow Knottingley A-B, Up and Down Goods Knottingley B-Depot West, Up and Down Goods Sudforth Lane-Whitley Bridge. An Up refuge siding at Streethouse West accommodated 34 wagons, engine and brake van.

A BR Appendix supplement dated May, 1970 recorded modernisation of signalling and conversion to Track Circuit Block. All signal boxes were abolished except Featherstone Stn., Knottingley Depot East(renamed Knottingley), Sudforth Lane and Hensall. Pontefract West Jn. came under the control of Prince of Wales box and Pontefract Goods Jn. under Knottingley. Streethouse West became a gatebox.

Local freight workings through Monkhill Mon-Sat 2.11.59-12.6.60

4.52am *pass*	4.20am Wakefield Withams Sdgs-Knottingley class H
6.13am *arr*	5.35 class F from Withams Sdgs.
10.21am *dep*	Class K to Knottingley
11.20-11.35	11.10 Knottingley-Wakefield Turner's Lane class K
3.41pm SO *pass*	2.41 Goole Sdgs-Turner's Lane class H
3.52-4.9pm SX	1.35 Goole Sdgs-Turner's Lane class H
3.59pm SO *pass*	3.50 Knottingley-Turner's Lane class H
7.18-7.42pm SX	6.5 Knottingley Depot-Turner's Lane class H
7.37-7.57pm SX	6pm Witham's Sdgs- Goole Beverley Sdgs Class K

Above: With Wilkinson's liquorice factory on the right, Aspinall 3F 0-6-0 No. 52244 passes Pontefract East box with a Goole to Wakefield pick-up in the late 1950s, the load including an open wagon on a well wagon. At this time there were five liquorice factories in Pontefract(there were once 13) but in 2002 there were only two while nowadays this entire view is completely obscured by trees. *Peter Cookson*

Below: Up and Down evening pick-up freights meet at Pontefract East in the late 1950s. The Up train has Aspinall 3F 0-6-0 No. 52305 in charge while the Down train in the yard is being worked by rebuilt version No. 52154. *Peter Cookson*

Above: Busy times at Monkhill station area in 1957. Class 2P 4-4-0 No. 40630 heads the 2pm Saturdays Only Wakefield-Goole away from the station as a 4F 0-6-0 stands in the goods yard on the left and a WD 2-8-0 in the sidings on the right. *Peter Cookson*

Below: A scene which soon became the norm in the area. In the 1960s during the early days of merry-go-round coal train working between local pits and the Aire Valley power stations, Knottingley-based Class 47 No. D1895 heads a train of 30 loaded 32-ton MGR wagons. The newish looking Shildon-built HAA-type hoppers, seen passing Pontefract goods yard, would soon be blackened by coal dust. In 2002 these ubiquitous wagons were being replaced by new high capacity bogie hoppers built in York. *Peter Cookson*

Above: Pontefract East Junction where the curve came up from Baghill station. Here a Derby lightweight DMU joins the Goole-Wakefield line while working a Baghill to Leeds Central service in 1961. The track bed of the curve and the viaduct it crossed are still there in 2002 but the view from Pontefract Monkhill-Knottingley trains is almost totally obscured by trees. *Peter Cookson*

Below: Half a mile further east is the curve down to Ferrybridge(described by the Sectional Appendix as the Ferrybridge Goods Branch) opened in 1965 to facilitate the movement of MGR coal trains to Ferrybridge power station. As can be seen here, it was also useful for other traffic such as this excursion to Bridlington for Featherstone Working Men's Club which was one of the last steam workings over the curve. The chalked reporting number 4F02 on the smokebox of Leeds Holbeck Black Five No. 44896 should be ignored, it is obviously left over from a previous working. Jubilee Junction where the curve, which has since been singled, leaves the Monkhill-Knottingley section is just round the bend out of sight. *Peter Cookson*

Above: Class 3F 0-6-0 No. 52273 blasts past the site of Jubilee Junction with a pick-up goods to Wakefield a good few years before construction of the curve down to Ferrybridge on the left. The scene is also before the M62 was built over the top of where the train is. *Peter Cookson*

Below: Following the removal of Knottingley station's overall roof in late 1966, a WD 2-8-0 hauls a load of coal Goole-bound through the station area and past Knottingley 'B' signal box. The present day station consists of two platforms with a waiting shelter and footbridge. *Peter Cookson*

Above and top of opposite page: Two views showing all the east end of Knottingley station in the mid to late 1950s. On the far left is the single road steam loco shed(demolished 1966), a sub-shed of Wakefield since closing as a depot in its own right in 1922. Knottingley 'B' signal box is situated in the 'V' between the lines from Askern approaching from the left and the Wakefield-Goole line running straight though the middle. A Class 2 2-6-0 runs under the bridge while shunting the goods yard on the right. *Both Peter Cookson*

David Holmes was assistant area manager(movements) at Knottingley from February, 1970 when the area management organisation came into being. "We had some fun to begin with, clearing out old station offices and finding all sorts of interesting documents including LNER green pea labels.

"There were many types of level crossings in the area, the L&Y ones tending to be staffed 24 hours a day by a lady living in an adjacent railway house. One old lady, "Ma" Bailey, retained her market pass from LMS days which enabled her to travel to the nearest town once a week, until the M62 cut the country lane and made her crossing redundant. Askern branch crossings were manned for two shifts by a man in a cabin. I asked one crossing keeper how often he had to open the gates to road traffic. He said: "See that bloke on a grey horse? Well, he crosses at least twice a day." This was the only regular use so arrangements were quickly made to withdraw attendance.

"Single Class 20 locos came from York to work coal and coke traffic. Certain depots had traditional areas and traffics. York worked coal from S&K collieries to Gascoigne Wood, Milford or Askern Coalite(York took this work over from Selby shed when it closed-ed.) Goole men took the shipping traffic, and Healey Mills men took general wagon-load traffic to Healey Mills yard.

"Kellingley Colliery kept our carriage & wagon men busy preventing hot axleboxes. This colliery would use BR wagons for internal traffic involving the tippler for which they were not designed and they lost oil from the axleboxes. I was in Streethouse signal box when a train from Kellingley passed with smoke coming from three wagons.

"The last shunting I ever did was at Pontefract Baghill. We were frequently short of a shunter and used to receive a train of bitumen each week when the M62 was being built. It was hard work, sorting out the empty railcars and then positioning the loaded ones. There were three sidings and different grades of bitumen had to go into each. A 6ft gap had to be left between each wagon so that heating could be applied to liquify the bitumen. It was a case of pin down brake on railcar, set loco back to ease the coupling, loose off, draw ahead 6ft, pin down then repeat the process again and again. I borrowed the Knottingley 08 area pilot for this job which took at least an hour of hard graft.

"In 1970 the Potato Marketing Board wanted to send a large quantity of surplus potatoes from Hensall to the West Country for cattle feed. My colleague Alan Johnson, the power station supervisor, said he could use the area pilot and a siding at Hensall station. It was stretching it a bit to expect the pilot to go there and back each day - quite a way at its slow speed - besides its other duties. But Alan was a chap who could fix anything and the job worked very well, 10 tons were loaded into each van and the vans brought back to Knottingley for forwarding to Healey Mills."

KNOTTINGLEY NOS.1 & 2 SIDINGS. Bogie coaches must not be placed in No.1 siding when bogie stock is standing in No.2 siding, nor must such vehicles be shunted into the latter road if No.1 siding is occupied with bogie vehicles. *LMS Sectional Appendix 1937 and BR NE Region Sectional Appendix 1960*

Below: Norton station, three and a half miles north of Shaftholme Junction where the branch from Knottingley joins the East Coast main line north of Doncaster, looking north in 1960, 13 years after it closed to passengers. Local goods traffic ceased in October, 1964. *Peter Cookson*

Above: One the slow freights which took the Askern branch to stay clear of the East Coast main line. Doncaster B1 4-6-0 No. 61365 heads past antique signals and through the half-demolished Norton platforms with a southbound class H Through Freight carrying a range of steel products.

Below: Another Doncaster engine passing a vintage signal, this time two and a half miles nearer Knottingley at Womersley station. No. 90651 is at the head of a northbound coal train bound for Crofton Hall sidings, near Wakefield, in 1957. Womersley was equipped to handle parcels and a full range of freight but the goods yard on the right, which had no permanent crane, closed in April, 1965. *Both Peter Cookson*

Above: If nothing else, this book should be memorable for the motive power variety within its pages and at last we have managed to get one of these in! A4 Pacific No. 60010 *Dominion of Canada* approaches Knottingley with the Sunday 11.15am King's Cross-Glasgow at 3.59pm on 16th April, 1961. Diversion of such expresses via Askern, Knottingley and Burton Salmon when the East Coast main line was blocked by engineering work was a regular event until the start of the 1990s. *David Holmes*

Below: A green field site, but not for much longer. WD 2-8-0 No. 90151 from 35A New England(Peterborough) shed approaches Knottingley from the Askern direction in 1956 with a class F unfitted express freight. In less than ten years the field on the left will have become the new diesel depot. *Peter Cookson*

Above: Just to the left of the previous picture, WD No. 90478 comes in from the Goole direction with a Through Freight, the diesel depot site on its right. *Peter Cookson*

As a fireman at Wakefield shed, Mr. B. Parr was, from 1956, loaned to Knottingley sub-shed to cover a morning and afternoon Leeds passenger service.

In a programme produced for a depot open day on 26th April, 1993, he recalled: "The freight side consisted of a two shift   travelling pilot which went all round Knottingley to three different glassworks. The afternoon turn had a run down to Askern at regular intervals delivering massive trees from South Wales for Askern sawmills.

"I transferred permanently to Knottingley in 1962. I was passed for driving in November but when I worked it out I realised that it would take me almost thirty years to get my first driving turns.

" Things were steady enough until the mid-Sixties when Knottingley was remodelled for layout and signalling. In 1965 we heard the first rumours about a steeply sloping field off Headlands Road being used as a new shed yard for Knottingley. "What a load of cobblers - they'll never get that down to railway level!" But when the diggers came in they soon did.

"I thought I would be made redundant but in 1966 we were packed off to York for diesel loco training and when we eventually got back to Knottingley the shed was working a few coal jobs into Ferrybridge power station.

"Other freight in the Sixties was local coal, sugar beet, peas and potatoes. The decline of the pea and potato trade started when the railway was only used to bring the empty sacks back to the farmers! Pollard Bearings factory at Ferrybridge called at the station with parcels to go by passenger train. A parcel about six inches square could easily weigh a quarter of a hundredweight.

"Live cattle and horses were brought into the Down side cattle dock for regular delivery to the local slaughter houses and we never went short of muck for our gardens.

"The biggest operational fright was for driver Bill Harrison blasting up the bank to Cridling Stubbs with a Hunslet 0-6-0 diesel mechanical loco and six loaded acid tanks. A crankpin cotter and collar came off and so did the side rod. Fortunately, you don't travel far at two and half miles an hour with one side of the locomotive up in mid air."

Knottingley diesel depot was built in 19966/67 and comprised a depot for maintenance and inspection of MGR wagons plus facilities for the inspection, maintenance and fuelling of diesel locomotives. Four 38-wagon trains could be inspected each day with wagons passing through the inspection shed in rakes of six.

Still a sub-shed of Wakefield, it was initially coded 56A but became 55G in 1968, taking the code of closed Huddersfield shed. Upon TOPS computerisation in 1973 it became KY.

Above: To be honest, the view of Knottingley diesel depot(left) and wagon depot(extreme right) hasn't changed dramatically since this view on 15th August, 1981. The BR blue livery of the Class 56s which had just replaced the Class 47s has given way to the red and gold of English Welsh & Scottish Railway while in 2003 the yard is just as likely to be full of much newer Class 60s and 66s. Since 1993 a big new train crew depot and management centre has dominated the scene behind the loco shed. *Adrian Booth*

To begin with in 1966, Knottingley diesel depot had 27 footplate staff and just two Class 47 locomotives working to Ferrybridge and Thorpe Marsh power stations from Frickley and South Kirkby Collieries. By 1978 the allocation had grown to 15 Class 47s(fitted with slow speed control for discharging hopper wagons at 0.5mph in power stations) plus three Class 08 shunters, but in summer, 1979 its main line fleet was real-located to Healey Mills - though still working from Knottingley. In May, 1980 the Class 47s were replaced by more powerful Class 56s. In about 1986, Healey Mills depot closed after which Knottingley's main line locos were supplied from the national Trainload Coal fleet based at Toton. Nowadays, they come from a regional fleet based at Immingham.

Left: A Class 08 diesel shunter receives attention inside Knottingley diesel depot in February, 1988. At this time, Knottingley's shunters were outbased from York. In 1989 the York allocation was run down and Nos. 08499 and 08777 were officially allocated to Knottingley. *Malcolm Roughley*

Locomotives allocated to 55G Knottingley, November, 1971: Class 47: 1890/1/2/3/4/5; Class 03 0-6-0 shunter: 2161/73; Class 08 350hp 0-6-0 shunter: 3379. Total: 9

Above: Heading out of Knottingley and towards Goole, WD 2-8-0 No. 90135 passes Knottingley Depot West signal box and a young audience as it approaches England Lane level crossing with a 1950s mineral train. *Peter Cookson*

Below: Looking east from the footbridge at England Lane at what nearly became an historic railway site as Trainload Coal Class 56 No. 56088 passes the former Knottingley Depot area with westbound empties on 6th March, 1993. The public delivery siding on the right has since been completely abandoned.

The L&Y Railway planned to build its locomotive works and wagon shops here and in the 1880s bought land to the right for that purpose. When it built the works at Horwich, Lancashire, instead, the land was used for a pickling shed where sleepers were soaked in creosote. In 2002 the site is occupied by the playing fields of Knottingley High School. *Steve Chapman*

Right: This home-made contraption, a 4-wheel diesel hydraulic loco built around 1972, was used at the Plasmor building blocks company in Womersley Road. Pictured there on 13th June, 1990, its job was to shunt five 4-wheeled trays of blocks at a time from the blockmaking plant to the autoclaves, needing five trips to fill an autoclave.

Plasmor's main line railhead is at Heck, between Selby and Doncaster.

Adrian Booth

The 1956 Stations Handbook showed Knottingley station goods depot as equipped with a 5 ton crane, being able to handle the full range of traffic. Knottingley Depot was a public delivery siding equipped with a 1 ton 10cwt crane and could handle general goods only. Local goods facilities were withdrawn in July, 1970.

It also listed the following private sidings: Bagley & Co. glassworks, Knottingley Depot; Crystal Glass Co. via Bagley's siding; Jackson Bros., near Knottingley station; and Yorkshire Tar Distillers, via Bagley's siding.

In 1981 it was noted that Bagley's works(then Rockware Glass) used an overhead monorail to carry sand from barges and a tractor to shunt its siding. Headlands Works(also Rockware) had a pair of Ruston diesels.

Above: Having come to grief at Knottingley Depot, J39 0-6-0 No. 64705 leans on a lean-to outbuilding of the railway house as a Goole-bound Metro-Cammell DMU creeps cautiously past. Nowadays, the whole line would probably be closed all day as a result of this.

Colour-Rail / Ernest Sanderson

Left: Smart-looking Sentinel 0-4-0 diesel hydraulic shunter NCB No. 111 (works No. 10120 of 1962) pictured on 24th October, 1975, was one of four similar locos at Kellingley Colliery. Connected to the Knottingley-Goole line just east of the town near Sudforth Lane, it is known locally as "Big K." A rapid loading bunker for MGR trains came into operation in 1981 but a standard gauge loco was still needed until 1991 to deal with house coal and the loading of containers.

"Big K" became the last deep mine in the area covered by this book when Prince of Wales closed. *Adrian Booth*

Below: Passing Sudforth Lane and the site of Whitley Bridge water troughs in the 1960s, Hull Dairycoates English Electric Type 3 No. D6735 takes a load of coal to Goole. The additional roads here are still used in 2003. *Peter Cookson*

WHITLEY BRIDGE: When an Up freight train is turned into Sudforth Lane loop between 8am and 5.30pm, and stops at the tank in the middle of the loop, the driver must obtain water as quickly as possible, and then proceed to Sudforth Lane signals so that Thornfields Crossing may be blocked as little as possible. Should a second train be turned into the loop at these times and be delayed behind the preceeding train, the guard of the second train must walk up to the crossing and divide his train, if necessary, to clear the crossing for vehicles or pedestrians. *LMS Central Division Sectional Appendix, 1937.*

In December, 1989 Ferrybridge power station received 17 incoming coal trains per 24 hours, from Murton, Frickley, Grimethorpe, Maltby, Kellingley and Goldthorpe pits. Eggborough received 23, from Harworth, Prince of Wales, Ollerton, Grimethorpe, Welbeck, Sharlston, Askern and Murton. Drax received 53, from Selby, Goldthorpe, Rossington, Maltby, Silverwood, Bentley, Easington, Dawdon and Sharlston.

Above: Whitley Bridge station as it was, looking towards Knottingley four and a half miles away, in the late 1950s - well kept with substantial buildings, all of which have since been swept away in favour of basic platforms and shelters. The large maltings belong to Associated British Maltsters. *Peter Cookson*

Below: As originally built in the 1960s, the Eggborough power station branch joined the Knottingley-Goole line by a triangular junction east of Whitley Bridge station, but the Goole-facing curve was subsequently abandoned. In this rare 1970s view, a Class 47 passes the junction with the already disused Goole curve while hauling empty MGR hoppers back from the power station to the main line. *David Cookson*

On Saturday 5th June, 1965 the biggest ever single railway load to that date left Ettingshall Road goods station, Wolverhampton, for Eggborough. Carried on two 24-wheel bogie wagons, the load was a 240-ton 122ft-long boiler for the new power station which was being built at the time.

The 1956 Stations Handbook showed Hensall equipped to handle general goods plus livestock, horse boxes and prize cattle vans. There was no permanent crane.

The towing of wagons by a locomotive on an adjacent line was permitted for moving them from the Up line to Robson's siding. Goods facilities survived here until 5th March, 1973.

Above: A typically grubby WD 2-8-0, too dirty to identify, clanks its way over the level crossing at Hensall station while heading in the direction of Knottingley in 1959. In the foreground is the goods dock while the station and main goods yard are behind the engine and brake van. The signal box, still in use in 2003, is on the right. The house on the left has since vanished. *Peter Cookson*

Below: Hensall station looking west in 1959. The scene is little different in 2003. The station remains beautifully kept and even the wooden shelter on the left survives even though the station became unstaffed as long ago as 1968. The semaphore signals have been replaced by colour lights, the crossing gates by booms and the bullhead track by modern flatbottom welded rail. The crossover has gone along with the goods yard but grounded goods vans have been placed in the caravan park behind the platform to give the impression that it is still there. Heavy coal and limestone trains still clatter through on their way to Drax power station and all Hensall lacks is a decent passenger service. *Peter Cookson*

Above: Having just passed under the East Coast main line east of Hensall station, a 1950s stopping passenger train from Wakefield makes its way to Goole hauled by 2P 4-4-0 No. 40630. Its next stop will be Snaith. To the right of the telegraph pole are the overgrown earthworks of a curve down from the East Coast main line which is thought never to have been used for normal traffic. *A. L. Brown / N. E. Stead collection*

Below: Hensall Junction looking towards Goole in October, 1966. The curve up to the Hull & Barnsley line, mothballed since the H&B closed in 1959, climbs away to the left. It was reopened in 1970 along with just over four miles of the H&B to carry coal trains serving Europe's biggest coal-fired power station at Drax.

A supplement to the 1972 Sectional Appendix issued in February, 1975 showed Hensall Junction as renamed Drax Power Station Branch Junction(since shortened to Drax Branch Junction) controlled from Hensall station signal box with Track Circuit Block signalling between Hensall and Snaith level crossing.

The Hull & Barnsley had an engine shed here for locomotives used on transfer traffic with the L&Y which once included passenger trains between Carlton Towers and Knottingley, and the remains can be seen on the left mostly obscured by trees.

In 2003, the double track continues up the Drax branch while a single line goes on to Goole carrying nothing but the very sparse passenger service. The signal box has gone. *Peter Rose*

Above: In the 1950s the fireman of 53A Hull Dairycoates WD 2-8-0 No. 90609 doffs his cap for the camera as his engine heads an eastbound class H Through Freight past Hensall Junction. The then reasonably intact and not so overgrown Hull & Barnsley engine shed stands proud on the right. *Peter Cookson*

Below: A little further east, one of 25A Wakefield shed's WDs, No. 90652, heads a long coal train underneath the Hull & Barnsley main line and towards Goole. *Peter Cookson*